HEROD
Reflections on Political Violence

Conor Cruise O'Brien

HEROD
Reflections on Political Violence

Hutchinson of London

Hutchinson & Co. (Publishers) Ltd
3 Fitzroy Square, London W1P 6JD

London Melbourne Sydney Auckland
Wellington Johannesburg and agencies
throughout the world

First published 1978

© Conor Cruise O'Brien 1978

Set in Monotype Bembo

Printed in Great Britain by
The Anchor Press Ltd and bound by
Wm Brendon & Son Ltd, both of
Tiptree, Essex

British Library CIP data

O'Brien, Conor Cruise
    Herod.
    1. Violence – Addresses, essays, lectures
    I. Title
    322.4'2   JC:

ISBN 0 09 133190

Contents

Introduction
The Legitimation of Violence

All the essays and lectures in this collection, with one exception, were written during the present decade, as was the last of the three plays, *King Herod Advises*. One essay, 'State Terrorism: The Calculus of Pain, of Peace and of Prestige', and the two other plays, *King Herod Explains* and *Salome and the Wild Man* are late products of the 1960s. They are also partly products of New York City, and of the protest movement in the American universities against the war in Vietnam.

I lived in New York from 1965 to 1969, having come there from Africa, where I spent most of the first half of that decade. Early in the decade – in 1961 – I had been responsible for the implementation, in Katanga – now the Shaba province of what is now Zaire and was then the Congo – of a United Nations Security Council Resolution which authorized 'the use of force if necessary in the last resort'. Force was used. Had it been necessary? Had the last resort been reached? In a book written immediately after these events – *To Katanga and Back* (1962) – I answered these questions confidently, politically, positively. In New York, six years later, I found myself answering them all over again, at a different level, in a play, *Murderous Angels*. The argument of that play concerned the legitimation of violence. That is also the theme of the three Herod plays in the second part of this collection and of the essays and lectures in the first part.

In New York, in the late 1960s, the debate about the legitimation of violence filled the air. The administration, and its supporters in the academies and in the media, sought to present their war in Vietnam as a justifiable response to Communist aggression and terrorism. This campaign of legitimation was backed by great resources, both financial and intellectual. But it had to be a campaign. Those who opposed the war – as I did – were free to speak. In the universities we used our freedom to expose what we saw as the sophistry of the arguments used in support of the war.* We sought, in fact, to *de-legitimize* the war, and our efforts met with some success.

At the same time, some of those who opposed America's war sought to use that opposition to legitimize other forms of violence. There was the waving of the Viet Cong flag and the burning of the American one. There were the slogans 'Burn, baby, burn' and 'Bring the war home'. In fact, these truculent manifestations were not accompanied by actual violence on a scale at all comparable to ordinary 'non-political' urban violence, or to guerrilla activity elsewhere, let alone to the actual war in Vietnam. But there were left-wing paramilitary and/or terrorist groups – the Black Panthers, the Weathermen–and both real and ostensible supporters of these groups did participate, with appropriate paraphernalia, in the great 'anti-war' rallies of the period. Their presence was, very naturally, used to discredit the anti-war movement generally – to de-legitimize the de-legitimizers. To those who wished to sit on the fence – perhaps a majority on the average university campus – these phenomena legitimized that particular posture: 'A plague on both your houses'. A student waving a Viet Cong flag in Washington Square became somehow equated with the napalming of Vietnam villages, and cancelled out that vision.

Like many another 'anti-war' university teacher at this time, I found myself conducting two different and somewhat contradictory sets of arguments, with two different sets of people. To the student left I was a 'right-winger', challenging their tendency to romanticize revolution and to idealize America's enemies – and especially their tendency to romanticize and idealize themselves. This side of the debate is reflected in some lines put into the mouth of Herod in *King Herod Explains*:

---

* In the present collection I have preserved only one out of many essays and lectures in this sense written at this time – 'State Terrorism: The Calculus of Pain, of Peace and of Prestige'.

VOICES: *Down with Herod the tyrant!*
Down with Herod the tyrant!

HEROD [grimly]: *The students are demonstrating –*
Demonstrating their righteousness,
But they really like me
Provided I use the appropriate Shibboleth –
Which of course I can do
As to the manner born.

At the same time, in public arguments with the 'fence-sitters' or 'plague on both your houses' school,* I found myself defending the position of the left-wing students, even to the point of idealizing and romanticizing that position. Hannah Ahrendt, with whom I debated at this time, has cited me as the author of the statement 'Violence is the only way of ensuring a hearing for moderation'. Strictly speaking, she had got the wrong O'Brien: that aphorism was coined by the nineteenth-century agrarian agitator William O'Brien. Yet I had quoted that statement, against the 'fence-sitters', with a degree of approbation which I find unjustifiable and repugnant in retrospect.

In this collection, *Salome and the Wild Man* represents the high water mark of the tendency to idealize the student revolution: and the moral purity – if not the intelligence – of the revolutionary.

In 1969 I returned to Ireland, as a Labour Member of the Irish Parliament. In Ireland the question of the legitimation of violence soon presented itself again, in a demanding and menacing fashion. The forms that that question has taken are reflected in most of the essays in this book, and in the final play, *King Herod Advises*. I do not want here to go over ground covered by the essays, the play or by my book *States of Ireland* (1972). It is, however, necessary to say something about the evolution of the writer's attitude towards the legitimation of violence, following his return to his own country.

---

* With the exception of a televised debate with William Buckley Jr I can recall no public discussions with unequivocally pro-Vietnam-war personalities. To do these latter justice, they would probably not have got a hearing on a big city campus, at this time. In the circumstances the 'fence-sitters' tended to carry the burden of the Establishment case.

Just as I brought to America the partly unresolved questions about the legitimation of violence, which had begun in United Nations service and in the Congo, so I brought back to Ireland the accumulation of questions on the same subject suggested by American as well as African experience; the African experience also now disturbingly increased by two visits to what was then 'Biafra' – the country of the Ibos – near the beginning and near the end of the Nigerian civil war.

The Ireland I came back to was mostly peaceful enough, as most of it still is. But the Civil Rights movement among the Catholics of Northern Ireland, and the attempts by Protestant vigilantes (including police vigilantes) to repress that movement had already shaken the foundations of Northern Ireland – a province in which a Protestant majority, cherishing the Union with Britain, had been in a position of dominance over a Catholic minority many, though not all, of whom aspired to be part of a united Ireland, separate from Britain.* In August 1969 the British Labour Government ordered the deployment of British troops to protect the Catholic population from Protestant repressive violence, which had taken a lethal form in Belfast. The Catholic population at that time welcomed the British troops and fraternized with them. But the IRA, and especially the Provisional IRA,† set themselves to break that fraternization, to promote hostility between the Catholics and the British, and to present themselves as liberators of the Catholics from those who had in fact intervened to protect them. And this in a province in which the Catholic minority, together with the gunmen who claimed to be liberating them, would be crushed by the armed forces of the Protestant majority, if the 'liberation' – involving the departure of the real protectors of the Catholic minority – ever took place.

I had sympathized with and given some small support to the Civil Rights movement in the days before the deployment of the British troops in August 1969. I was aware that while that movement was in itself non-violent it was likely to provoke violence. I wrote about the situation in Derry in 1968 as 'frozen violence'. In itself this was accurate enough. The situation in Derry City was

* For Catholic attitudes see below, 'Northern Ireland Observed'.
† For the IRA see below, 'American Aid to Freedom-Fighters?' and *passim.*

then an undemocratic one, in which a Protestant minority (in the city) ruled over a local Catholic majority with the aid of a Protestant police force. But I did not give adequate attention to what would be likely to happen when all that violence *unfroze*. How many children is it worthwhile to kill to get rid of Derry Corporation?

What happened was that Derry Corporation, the old Stormont itself, and the institutions of caste supremacy generally, all disappeared, and people went on killing children and others, and legitimizing the killing of children and others. In the Republic of Ireland, where I lived, people sincerely deplored the violence in the North, and also persisted in using language that legitimized that violence.* Two of the three Dublin morning papers, one Sunday newspaper, and the solitary Dublin 'intellectual' periodical regularly published material tending to legitimize the existence and objective of the Provisionals – never of course any specific tactic of theirs. Ireland's right to unity; the corresponding non-right of the Northern Ireland majority to have a state of their own; the deluded and ridiculous nature of that majority; the baseness of the British, the absurdity of their institutions and the brutality of their forces; the identification of Irish patriotism with anti-British feeling – these were the dominant assumptions of this press and of the vein of tribal self-righteousness which it fed, and on which it fed. Reading this stuff anyone who had lived among other tribes for any length of time had to feel choked with the sense of *déjà vu* and *déjà entendu* and with the sheer implacable, impenetrable cosiness of it all. 'Of course we are right; are we not always telling ourselves so?' What was most oppressive was not the legitimation of violence in itself, but the frivolity of this legitimation, the refusal to see that it was legitimation, or that legitimation was important. 'Violence is a by-product of the partition of our country' is a statement by a political leader – Mr Jack Lynch, now Taoiseach – who has often and sincerely condemned the IRA. But if you tell him that in that and similar statements he and his friends have provided the IRA with its charter of legitimacy, and that it is a sense of legitimacy which sustains a fighting force and keeps up the killing, then he will

---

* See below, 'King Herod Explains', 'Shades of Republicans', etc.

look at you with those hurt eyes: 'How can you say that of me?'

It is not contended in these essays that the legitimation of violence (force) is always wrong. It is contended that the legitimation of violence (force) as a lesser evil in any particular circumstances is a profoundly serious matter which has to be capable of being established and defended on rational grounds, in relation to those circumstances, if it is to have any moral force. Legitimation by play on the emotions, by obliquity, by scientism, by appeal to tribal self-applause and atavistic resentments, has no moral force, but it can have considerable political force.

I have spent, as this collection partly testifies, some time in attempting to dismantle legitimation-structures of that kind. Some of them were legitimation-structures of a kind which had once impressed me. The confrontation-seeking 'left wing' of the Civil Rights movement* modelled itself on the left wing of the anti-Vietnam-war student movement in America and later on the French student revolution (just as the Northern Irish civil rights movement generally had modelled itself earlier on the civil rights movement in Dixie). This was impressive to the author of *Salome* although the author of *King Herod Explains* had to have his doubts. These doubts crystallized into certainties after returning to Ireland, and especially on contemplating the behaviour of these left-wingers after the deployment of British troops in August 1969 – an event which inevitably signalled the end of the old institutionalized caste system in Northern Ireland (Derry Corporation and the rest.) But the 'left-wingers' now emerged as the agitational arm of the IRA in converting what had been ostensibly a civil rights campaign (whose essential objectives had been achieved) into an overtly nationalist campaign directed both against the British and against all who favoured the British connection – virtually all Protestants in Northern Ireland. The ginger group called 'People's Democracy', which had been at the core of the 'civil rights left wing', now provided the Provisional IRA with propaganda designed to make those Catholic soldiers look presentable to left-wing extremists in other countries; the Provos themselves could look after the business of collecting the money from right-wing Catholic Irish-Americans.

This movement had in fact turned its 'non-sectarian', 'inter-

* See 'A Yankee at the Court of Queen Bernadette'.

national', 'class-centred' rhetoric into material for the legiti-mation of tribal civil war in Northern Ireland.*

As for me, that was precisely what I wanted to de-legitimize, shedding some friends and some illusions in the process. In the politics of the Republic I was not quite where I was expected to be. In the Congo time, sections of the British press had assured their readers (quite wrongly) that I was motivated by anti-British fanaticism. My career in America had shown me as opposed to imperialism. So I was expected at least to fall into line with the view that the troubles of Northern Ireland were caused by British imperialism. When instead I said that, in relation to Northern Ireland, it was the IRA who were the imperialists, since they were trying to annex by force a territory a large majority of whose inhabitants were opposed to them, my remarks appeared either incomprehensible or outrageous to a number of people who had liked what they heard *about* me much more than they like what they were hearing *from* me.

My statements incurred for me intense unpopularity in certain limited circles, and a milder degree of unpopularity in wider circles. Politically speaking, it was the milder degree which was the more dangerous. People who dislike anything to do with violence do not like to be reminded that their own habitual assumptions may be feeding the violence. Politicians are unwise to remind people who have votes of things they do not wish to be reminded of. This consideration may or may not have had something to do with the loss of my Dail seat in the summer of 1977. Those who 'condemned, but legitimized' on the other hand won. Yet in doing so they laid no stress on their legitimations. They said Northern Ireland was not an issue in the elections. Of course it had to be an issue if they had meant what they had said about it – they had called for a British commitment to withdraw, which the then Government of the Republic had refused to call for. But it was not an issue: the drums were muffled; the legiti-mations kept in the shadows. It may be, and I think it is, the case that people are both increasingly uncomfortable about the legitimations, and impatient with those who have helped to make them uncomfortable. If so, the discomfort at least represents a measure of progress.

* See 'A Global Letter'.

PART ONE
Reflections on
Political Violence

A Global Letter

Howth
Dublin
Ireland

February 1972

Dear . . .

No doubt we do live, as McLuhan says, all in the one 'electronic village'. But we continue at the same time, much more than men like McLuhan and Koestler have supposed, to inhabit our pre-electronic villages: national, local, tribal.

I am writing to you from one such village, at a time when that village has particular reason to question its relations with the rest of the world. I am myself a man who has lived much outside my village – in America and in Africa – and has had reason to question my relation to my village, and to the world outside.

I want to tell you about some of these questions, asking you to bear with their particularity – even a parochial particularity – in the hope that at some point the questions, and such beginnings of answers as I think I find, may link with questions and answers of your very different 'villages', and that we may begin to help one another through this correspondence.

What exactly is my village?

Dublin is the capital of the Republic of Ireland. With that

Contribution to a series of such letters organized by *Forum*.

simple statement, for us, the questions begin. The Republic of Ireland, as far as the outside world is concerned, is a state, 95 per cent of whose inhabitants are Roman Catholic, whose territory covers five-sixths of the island of Ireland – the remaining sixth being Northern Ireland, a part of the United Kingdom of Great Britain and Northern Ireland.

For most of us citizens of the Republic in our daily lives and more prosaic frames of mind, that is also pretty well how it is. Yet the Republic, proclaimed in Easter Week 1916, claimed to be the whole island of Ireland, with all its inhabitants. The Constitution of our existing Republic also claims right of jurisdiction over the entire island. Furthermore, this claim is generally felt to be valid among the Catholics who make up rather more than one-third of Northern Ireland's population. And a number of young men, brought up on this claim – which denies all legitimacy to the entity known as Northern Ireland – are using arms to make the claim good. If these young men are told that they have no mandate from the people for this recourse to violence – and they have no such mandate – they ask what mandate had the tiny minority of men who rose in arms in Easter Week 1916, in defiance not only of England, but of all the elected representatives of the Irish people, North and South? It is extremely hard to find an effective answer to this point within the framework of the 'official' culture of the Republic, for which the Easter Rising belongs virtually to the sphere of the sacred, its wisdom hardly more open to question than the dogmas of the Church. But the young men have other points to make. It was the threat of force – Protestant force – by the Ulster Volunteer movement of 1912–14 which created Northern Ireland as a separate entity. Why may not that which was created by force be challenged by force? Again, the more sophisticated spokesmen of physical force present the argument of 'institutionalized violence'. Where there is social injustice, enforced by law, then violence is diffused throughout the institutions of the state, and it is hypocritical to object (or to object *only*) to *illegal* acts of violence, which are no more immoral than the legal ones at which we daily connive. (The trouble with this argument, theoretically the most formidable of the three, is that it serves to justify violence which is *not* happening more than violence that *is* happening: the unemployed man in the Republic, who receives far lower unemployment benefit and family allowances than the unemployed man in Northern Ireland (which shares in the British welfare state), is thus a greater victim of institutionalized violence, yet has not in fact resorted to overt violence in return.)

We are thus forced to think, in our village – whatever its exact boundaries – about the relation of violence to our prevailing myths, to our past history, and to the condition of our society.

We are being forced to think about these things not primarily by arguments but by the fact of violence itself, by the impact of the reports and the images of violence: the face of a typist disfigured by flying glass; a child's head blown off while he slept; a woman blinded by a rubber bullet: another woman tarred and feathered, her head shaved; fifteen people bombed to death in a pub; thirteen young men shot dead in a street.

These were not the acts of ordinary criminals, but of men adhering to differing concepts of legitimacy and justice.

In these conditions the ethnic and cultural frontiers that traverse the electronic village become perceptible. People see the same images, hear the same words, but feel so differently about them that they cease to be the same. Almost all Catholics saw the young men shot dead by British paratroopers on 30 January in Derry as innocent victims wantonly murdered: most Ulster Protestants saw the same men as terrorists, or at best hooligans, whose death was a necessary part of the restoration of order, in a community which such men wished to destroy.

I have seen in other parts of the world – in Nigeria especially, during the civil war – that strange and terrible concentration of tribal feeling, through which members of the hostile tribe cease to appear as human, and become legitimate targets for any kind of violence. I have seen and am seeing manifestations of this now in my own village. I have witnessed the ceremony of the crying out of the names of the patriot dead: those who invoked the dead seeming, like mediums, in the grip of some outside force, and communicating a part of that force: those listening, partly under the spell, partly embarrassed and uncomfortable, but mostly overawed. At times I have felt that I was living in that Ionesco play in which each of the characters, one after another, turns into a rhinoceros. It is not as bad as that, or not yet, or not South of the border. Given half a chance, people have ways of resisting the spell of the dead and of blood: often devious ways, of inconsequence, of inconsistency, of routine, of well-spaced silences, meaningless remarks, hearty but perfunctory agreement followed by a swift change of subject – logically despicable devices no doubt, but important in humanity's defences against fanaticism. I have seen men and women, who seemed for a moment seriously to contemplate a career as a rhinoceros quietly drop the idea. The worst, as Claudel said, is not always the most certain.

Many of you who will be reading this are statistically in considerably greater danger of violent death than the writer is. I believe more people met violent death in New York last year than in Northern Ireland, let alone the relatively peaceful Republic. What is peculiar in our situation at present is the need to think about *legitimate* violence – violence, that is, which can be seen as legitimate in terms of dominant assumptions within the society – while knowing that that kind of violence is frequent, fairly widely condoned, near to hand, and unpredictable in its further manifestations.

In these conditions one tends to look again at such a concept as 'institutionalized violence', and in particular at the use of such a concept to legitimize overt acts of illegal violence.

As far as our village is concerned, it is true, 'institutionalized violence' is a much less potent concept for purposes of legitimation than are prevailing myths of history and the cult of the dead. But it is through such concepts as 'institutionalized violence' that the more antique and atavistic parts of the repertoire of legitimation *are themselves legitimized* in the minds of, for example, students and ex-students, and of others who would be ashamed to think of themselves as obsessed by the past. And it is through such concepts, and through those who find comfort in them, that our forms of violence come to seem legitimate internationally, and especially among the international left.

It is quite true that violence is institutionalized in all forms of organized society. Only an anarchist, only a man or woman who would in no circumstances invoke the law or call in the police, can consistently claim the name of pacifist.

It is also true that, since all forms of organized society that we know – or that man ever has known – contain great inequalities of power, wealth and status, and since these inequalities are in the last resort defended by violence, anyone who lives in any such society, and accepts its rules, is condoning some degree of oppressive violence.

From a recognition of these facts, it is an easy step to repudiate as hypocrisy the attitude of those who condemn the violence of the terrorist, the rural or urban guerrilla, without equally condemning the institutionalized violence of the society which the terrorist is trying to destroy, in order to rebuild. It is even easy to exonerate the terrorist completely from *all* responsibility, and see the society as responsible not only for the blood it sheds, itself, but for the blood it drives its enemies to shed. The terrorist who plants a bomb in a supermarket is (on this argument) not responsible for the resulting deaths of women and children: it is the supermarket itself, the values it represents, and the laws which defend those values, which are responsible.

This is the argument of those who defend the IRA – and similar organizations – on a high moral plane, reasoning from a kind of ultra-pacifism right out to the acceptance of indiscriminate terrorism. Some clergymen, both Catholic and Protestant, have travelled this road, or a long stretch of it. Some political friends of the terrorists have shown themselves adroit at exploiting this line of argument. It serves in various forms to anaesthetize public sensibilities after each new killing. Not everybody, of course, is up to the general theory of institutionalized violence. But most people can find significance in such a statement as, for example, 'violence is a by-product of partition'. The significance found by simpler, ruder spirits is that, when a Protestant is killed by a Catholic, he had it coming to him. This is the extended doctrine of institutionalized violence as seen at grass-roots level, for institutionalized violence in Northern Ireland has long been a Protestant monopoly. The other kind of violence is practised by both sides.

The existence of institutionalized violence is a fact. The use of that fact to justify terrorism requires an act of faith: the conviction that the society resulting from the terrorist's activities will not merely be better than the existing one, but better by such a margin as to justify the killing of an indefinite number of people. As evidence that this will be the case, the terrorist can only offer, first, the undoubted fact of his willingness to sacrifice his own life (as well as those of other people) and, second, manifestos which describe, in rosy terms, the society he says he intends to bring to being. Neither piece of evidence can be wholly convincing to anyone who remembers the career, underground and overground, of Joseph Stalin.

Only extreme circumstances can justify such an act of faith. Examples of such extreme circumstances are the manifest failure and disintegration of formerly organized polities – as in Russia and China – and the existence of such conditions for whole communities – Jews in the Third Reich, to a lesser extent non-Whites in South Africa – that no possible alternative seems likely to be worse,★ while no peaceful method of changing the existing conditions is open. In all these cases the new forms of institutionalized violence, resulting from anti-institutional violence, seem at least less unpromising than the old ones.

Did such conditions exist in Northern Ireland? It is argued that they did. The Catholics of Northern Ireland were and are in a permanent minority in what has always been run as a Protestant state. They were second-class citizens, discriminated against in jobs and housing, and often obliged to emigrate. Since the Protestant majority always voted virtually *en bloc* for the Unionist Party, perpetrator of the discriminations in question, ordinary democratic process offered no hope for the Catholic minority.

All this is true. What is not true is the idea that terrorism, the urban guerrilla, therefore represented the only way out – or *any* way out – for the Catholic minority.

The Catholics lived within a double system: they were part of Northern Ireland, and also of the larger entity, the United Kingdom. In so far as they were part of Northern Ireland they were oppressed to the degree described; in so far as they were part of the United Kingdom, they received their fair share of the benefits of the welfare state. Their legitimate complaint against the successive Governments of the United Kingdom was that these Governments had condoned, by ignoring, the oppressive practices in Northern Ireland, much as the Government in Washington had ignored the peculiar institutions of Dixie,

★This may not be true for South Africa's 'Coloureds' and 'Asians', and even for at least some 'Bantu'.

from the end of Reconstruction up to Little Rock in 1957. By far the most promising and most effective way of dealing with this situation was through the non-violent agitation, for limited objectives, of the Civil Rights movement. As in Dixie, this kind of agitation evoked violence on the part of the locally dominant party and, as in the case of Dixie, the spectacle of this violence, and the knowledge of what it represented, were unacceptable in the wider society. The continuation of this movement, therefore, represented by far the best hope of removing the disabilities of the Catholic community. The coming of the urban guerrilla had the opposite effect: it alienated sympathies, sharply increased the hostility between the two communities and put the minority in double jeopardy: first from the British troops, which see the minority as harbouring those who attack them, and second from the Protestant majority, much of which has been driven to near-hysteria by the ruthlessness of the urban guerrilla, and especially the use of gelignite against civilian targets. If the British troops were suddenly withdrawn, without a negotiated political solution, one of the first results of their withdrawal would be the destruction of the Catholic population of the Belfast area – of whom the terrorists claim to be the defenders. Yet, as long as the British troops remain, and the guerrilla war against them continues, the Catholic community will also be the prime sufferers. The best hope of this community lies, in fact, in the disappearance from the scene of their 'defenders', and in a complete and consistent return to open and peaceful methods, leading to new negotiated structures and to the withdrawal of the British troops. There are some signs of a trend in that direction, both North and South of the border, but it is too early to be sure, even of the beginning of a trend.

We can't, without hypocrisy, claim to rule out now all violence, either inside human institutions or as a means for changing them. We can continue to try to reduce the incidence of violence in both senses. This means *both* greater activity in the criticism and peaceful change of our institutions, *and* a no less critical and suspicious attitude towards those who offer change by violence. In particular we should be suspicious of those who would justify terrorism through the concept of institutionalized violence.

Liberty and Terror

The situations I should like to discuss with you are those in which democratic governments, working under the rule of law, are confronted by armed revolutionary organizations seeking to attain political objectives by the use of violence, and through the terror which violence inspires.

In such struggles, each side sees itself as upholding the cause of liberty, but the idea of liberty is differently defined by each side, and with widely different degrees of precision.

Supporters of the democratic system – be they conservative, liberal or social-democrat supporters – see that system as providing more effective guarantees of liberty, and a more effective demonstration of liberty in action, than any other known political system. The guarantees are seen to reside, not only in the electorate's periodically available capacity to change its political rulers, but more importantly in the permanent necessity under which these rulers find themselves to try to please a majority of the ruled, and also in the further constraints placed on the rulers by the legal system, by the independence of the judiciary, and by the accredited values and conventions of the liberal and democratic tradition. There is no need at this point to enlarge on these conceptions: presumptions in favour of democracy are taken for granted, rightly or wrongly, among populations which enjoy, in varying degrees, that form of government. Praise of democracy therefore readily enters into the domain of platitude, which is itself among the dangers to democracy, especially in lowering its appeal to the young. I mean, of course, the young who grew up within the democratic system: young people who have grown up under

The Cyril Foster Lecture at the University of Oxford, 6 May 1977.

other systems often seem quite attracted to the democratic idea.

For the moment, the only point I should like to make about the version of liberty offered by the liberal and democratic state is that, however we choose to view the virtues and vices of that version of liberty, people who live in democratic states know what that version means in practice to them. The equivalent is true of those who live under other different but existing systems of government: the Soviet Union, for example, has its own version of liberty and those who live under that system know from experience how to evaluate that version.

But the same is *not* true of the versions of liberty offered by those who like to call themselves 'liberation movements' and who, as they seek to establish their version of liberty by violence and terror, are called by their enemies 'terrorists'. 'Terrorists' is of course an emotive term, used to describe people seen as making an *unjustifiable* use of violence. Those who are described as terrorists, and who reject that title for themselves, make the uncomfortable point that national armed forces, fully supported by democratic opinion, have in fact employed violence and terror on a far vaster scale than what liberation movements have as yet been able to attain.* The 'freedom-fighters' see themselves as fighting a just war. Why should they not be entitled to kill, burn and destroy as national armies, navies and air forces do, and why should the label 'terrorist' be applied to them and not to the national armies, navies and air forces?

Some pacifists – and not only pacifists – have found the argument implicit in these questions exceedingly impressive. Pacifists put the formal argument the other way round: instead of both national armies and freedom-fighters/terrorists having an equal right to kill, both are equally wrong to do so. Some pacifists, and some who are not quite pacifists, have pushed this argument to what does in fact appear to be its logical conclusion – that the national security forces, even in a democracy, have no right to repress armed minority groups pursuing political objectives by violent means. The minority groups, it is true, don't have the right to use such means, but both are on the same footing. In practice, the view is helpful to the minority groups in question,

*See below, 'State Terrorism: The Calculus of Pain, of Peace and of Prestige'.

so that people passionately opposed in principle to violence, and people passionately devoted to its practice, can sometimes be brought into a strange alliance.

In point of intellectual principle – though not in practice – the freedom-fighter/terrorists and those who support the use of force against them by the agents of the democratic state, have more in common than either group has with the pacifist. In practice, as I have indicated, the bond may join pacifist and terrorist, but intellectually there is this much common ground between the two groups which are prepared to use force, to the extent that circumstances are thought to justify its use.

Through the theme of justification we come back to the question of liberty, the value in the name of which both the force or violence of the terrorist/freedom-fighters, and the force or violence used by the democratic state in the suppression of the terrorist/freedom-fighters, can be seen as justified. The terms 'force' and 'violence' are again, like 'terrorist' and 'freedom-fighter', largely emotive propaganda terms: which term we use about a given act depends, not on the degree of force or violence involved, but on a view of its justification.

Those who regard the democratic state as justified in using force in defence of liberty may not be able to offer a philosophically satisfactory definition of liberty, but at least they have practical experience of the conditions which they identify as constituting political liberty, for themselves and their fellow-citizens, and which they consider to be of sufficient value to justify the use of force in the defence of something known and held to be precious.

As against this, the concept of liberty offered by the liberation movements lacks an identifiable terrestrial referent. Those who are inclined to identify terror with Communism might disagree with this. But it does not appear that most of those groups at present using violence in democratic countries are doing so in order to replace democratic systems by states on the Russian or Chinese models. Were that to be the goal, there would at least be a basis for the assessment of the version of liberty offered by the liberation movement in question. As it is, no such reliable basis of assessment is available – only 'programmes' and other forms of propaganda.

The versions of liberty offered by the various liberator/terrorists can be roughly divided into two main categories: millenarian and secessionist/irredentist. The two categories overlap, since the secessionist/irredentist militants present a millenarian picture of the results which they believe would flow from the alienation or recuperation of their territory of predilection.

This local millennium is of course indispensable, as the result supposedly aimed at has not merely to be presented, but also to be felt, as justifying killing, maiming, burning and other forms of destruction. The mere achievement of some desirable regional adjustment could not be presented or felt as justifying all that, so higher, quasi-mystical versions of a conditional future articulate themselves. Although the two categories do thus appear to overlap, yet a distinction can still be made between the true or universal millenarians, and those whose intensely limited mystical nationalism uses millenarian language in a particular and local context.

Examples of true millenarian movements include the Weathermen and the Symbionese Liberation Army in the United States and the Baader Meinhof group in Germany. Examples of ultra-nationalist movements, with millenarian overtones, include the various Arab militant groups which aim at liberating Palestine by destroying Israel, and the various Irish Republican groups, of which the most notable is the Provisional IRA which aims at liberating Northern Ireland against the known wishes of the majority of its inhabitants, and by methods strongly condemned by the great majority both of the population of Northern Ireland and of all Ireland, as well as of the United Kingdom.

There are also cases where a local conflict is felt as having universal significance. The most obvious example is that of the Zionist terrorist/liberators whose campaign was felt to have a religious and moral significance for the whole world. But, in a secular way, the American groups see their particular struggles as struggles for or against America in the interests of the whole world. And in both secular and religious terms the Provisional IRA are disposed to see their fight as having a world significance, and to think of God as especially concerned with Irish history, and as keeping a particularly attentive and discriminating eye on those 'dreary steeples' of Tyrone and Fermanagh which so irritated Winston Churchill and so many others since his time.

The millenarian and particularist forms of liberation/terrorism are therefore distinguishable but often interlocking. What exactly are the concepts of liberty for which these two groups are prepared to sacrifice so much, and so many?

It is very difficult, indeed probably impossible, to answer this question. In some cases, the movements concerned either acknowledge, or scarcely bother to hide, the fact that they have no programme at all. Thus the Italian movement known as the Autonomi has been quoted as rejecting discussion of programmatic goals and simply stressing 'vitality and action'. In this case it is not a question of using terror to achieve some version of liberty in the future. Terror *is* liberty, here and now. It is not altogether surprising that such a doctrine should come to us out of the cradle-land of Fascism. Yet if other terrorist/liberation movements were equally frank I think many of them, and certainly many individual participants in them, would have the same message to convey. With few exceptions, terrorists are not theorists, or interested in theory. The few who wish to articulate general ideas, and are capable of doing so in writing, are often taken by outsiders as 'speaking for' the movement. In fact the business end of the movement – the killers and potential killers – may know little and care less about what these putative spokesmen are saying. Thus the IRA in the 1960s came to be regarded as a Marxist movement, mainly because one highly articulate Marxist intellectual had a considerable influence over the 'Chief of Staff'. The programme and propaganda of the movement took on a distinctly Marxist tinge. But in 1969 it became clear that many members – including the most dangerous ones – were not interested in the ideology of their spokesmen. The Provisional IRA,* opting for violence in the here and now, was not a new entity; it consisted of people who had been deemed to be spoken for by intellectuals who were not in fact speaking for them. The Provisionals in their turn produced their own programme – a purportedly democratic socialist and federalist document – and their own intellectuals. Of the latter an Irish

*The 'Provisionals' broke with the 'Official' IRA leadership late in 1969. Spokesmen for the 'Officials' continue to use Marxist language.

wit has said that they have minds like unripe gooseberries: 'small, bitter, fuzzy and green'.

This programme, and the public utterances of these intellectuals, have probably even less relevance to the realities of the movement than had their equivalents in the IRA of the 1960s. At a Republican social gathering a few years back someone referred respectfully to the Provisionals' most prominent political spokesman. 'Him?' said a veteran contemptuously. 'When did *he* last "do" a British soldier?' The veteran was, I believe, more relevant than the propagandist: head-hunting the truth behind the talk of federalism.

Intellectuals, being by definition interested in words and ideas, are more likely to be misled about the reality of such movements than are ordinary people. Intellectuals are apt to scrutinize the programmes and manifestos of such movements in the hope of learning about their nature, without suspecting that they might perhaps learn as much about that matter from studying a bus ticket or the entrails of a crow as from such documents.

The man in the street, who is much less interested in the latest manifesto than in the latest explosion, is also much closer to the realities and priorities of the movements themselves. The unreality of stated aims is more obvious in the case of the millenarian /universalist type of movement, than in the territorial secessionist/ irredentist type.

The millenarians aim at destroying the existing structure of society, at bringing down 'the whole great guilty temple'. They assume, or appear to assume, that what would replace a bombed-out capitalism or Communism would be a new and ideal form of society. There are no rational grounds for such an assumption, but millenarians are interested in faith, not reason. Because their objective is so fantastic, because it is obviously incapable of being met by any concessions, and because this attempt to achieve the impossible by violence puts us *all* at risk, there is relatively little public inclination – though there is some – to try to meet these particular terrorists halfway.

It is otherwise with the territorial terrorists. Their versions of liberty are, or appear to be, attainable, and even relatively modest: the transfer of a particular territory, the withdrawal of particular forces. And those who would be inconvenienced by these transactions seem to be limited in number: some Jews here, some Protestants there, perhaps some Catholics too. There are those – not being Jews, or that kind of Protestant or Catholic, or resident in the area scheduled for liberation – who think, not always aloud, that all that might not be too high a price for the cessation of a terror that endangers, for example, all airline traffic.

It is to those who may think like that that the terrorist is addressing himself, after his own peculiar fashion.

The most obvious difficulty about concessions to territorial violence is that such concessions are liable to excite counter-violence from other claimants to the disputed territory. The most active territorial terrorists today are Irish and Arab claimants to territories in which the existing local population rejects the violent claimants by a large majority. In such cases it appears inevitable that concessions to territorial terror would result in counter-terror on a greater scale, flowing from a larger and more bitterly resented grievance. Even without such concessions, the mere existence of revolutionary terror is likely to generate the counter-terror of the vigilante, aiming either at maintaining the status quo, or restoring some status quo of the recent past. But actual concessions to revolutionary terror make the vigilante backlash much harder to contain and accelerate the cycle of the competing terrors.

And if that massive difficulty were not enough, there is the further difficulty that what looks to the outsider like a limited territorial claim is liable to take on much more cloudy and ominous forms in the minds of the terrorists themselves, and may in fact be quite as unreal and unattainable as the demands of the universalists. There is, as I indicated earlier, a millenarian aspect also to territorial terrorism. This is rather clearly visible in the case of the demands of the IRA. Many Northern Unionists, and many people in Britain too, think the IRA want Northern Ireland to be handed over to the Dublin Government. But that is not at all what the IRA want, either formally or substantially. For them, the Dublin Government is a vassal government of England's, the Dublin parliament a vassal parliament. The fact that the parliament is democratically elected is irrelevant.

The Republic for which they think of themselves as fighting is not the internationally recognized entity known as the Republic of Ireland. Their Republic – the Republic of the Republicans – is more like Plato's Republic in that it is an ideal, never achieved and never likely to be achieved. It requires total separation from Britain – in Wolfe Tone's often-repeated words, 'to break the connection with England, the never failing source of all our political evils'. The connection is most clearly seen in Northern Ireland, which is why that target has priority at present. But, for the IRA, Dublin has not broken the connection either. There is unfinished business there too. The connection must be totally broken, and obviously the existing state preserves and fosters many links with Britain, economic, social, cultural, linguistic and even (through the EEC) political. For the Republican such links represent a disguised form of the old imperialism. The connection has not been broken. As the Social and Economic Programme of Provisional Sinn Fein states: 'The nature of the connection goes much deeper than simply the occupation by foreign troops.' Nor is it just the connection with Britain which is intolerable: any connection with a Western Europe which includes Britain has also to be fought. The same document says that 'Sinn Fein will resist and oppose Brussels domination just as the Irish people have resisted British domination for centuries.' The 'Irish people' does not here mean the actual population of Ireland, as a casual reader might perhaps assume. The actual people of Ireland – *this generation* of that people, in the Republican vocabulary – are not thought of as having the right to say whether the connection has or has not been broken.

The arbiters of whether Wolfe Tone's ideal has been achieved are the faithful few, the pure Republicans, in short the IRA. Their demand is not merely for a limited territorial concession, it is for *Eire Nua*: A New Ireland. The achievement of that New Ireland would, I think, require two rather basic changes for the island of Ireland: a new geographical location and a new population. These may prove difficult either to negotiate or to extort by physical force.

I have spoken in a little detail of this particular territorial-millenarian demand because it is the one whose consequences most directly concern both you and me, and because it is the one with which I am most familiar. But I believe that other revolutionary territorial-terrorist groups are likely to show a significant number of similar characteristics: an exalted and unrealistic conception of their objective, a contempt for ordinary people and for what such people are prepared to accept as satisfactory or tolerable, and the conception that willingness to use force constitutes the qualification to be the arbiter of the result.

The claim is made that the state of whose Government I am a member* – the Republic of Ireland – owes its existence to territorial terrorism, and to negotiation by the British Government of that time with the terrorists. I reject that claim. Basically our state owes its existence to the known and attested demand of a majority of its inhabitants for self-government and to the recognition, in Britain and the world, of the legitimacy of that demand. That demand was repeatedly expressed at the polls; it was also expressed by violent means.

The men with whom Lloyd George negotiated in 1921 were all elected representatives and members of a political party with a large majority in the territory on which the state which emerged from the negotiations was based. That democratic and representative capacity – not the rather meagre armed force behind them – was the real strength of their position. And when they had negotiated their new state – which was identical in territory with that offered by the Liberal Government before the war, and before the use of any Irish violence – they then had to defend it against the pure Republicans and the pure gunmen, indifferent then as now to the democratic concept. Nor is that struggle yet over.

The idea of negotiating with men who have no democratic base, and no democratic mandate or responsibility, whose sole passport to the negotiating table is the gun, is a quite different matter. I am speaking, of course, of conditions in which democratic consultations are regularly and normally available, as in these islands. It seems to me that, in these conditions, democratic governments cannot, without abdication of trust and a fruitless abdication at that, engage in political negotiations with people whose sole claim to take part in such negotiations is their proven capacity to kill, burn or destroy and whose objectives in such negotiations are incapable of fulfilment. The record of democratic governments themselves, in relation to violence, is far from

*The Coalition Government of 1973–7.

spotless, but this fact does not negate the progress in civilization which government responsible to the governed represents, nor does it require or entitle the heirs of democracy to surrender any part of that heritage to an arbitrary power deriving solely from the barrel of a gun. On this view, the *force* used by a democratic state against the terrorist is legitimate, while the *violence* of the terrorist is not legitimate. I am deliberately now using the vocabulary which goes with the concept of legitimacy which I hold, and for which I argue here.

It may seem to some of you that the results of this analysis are so obvious as scarcely to require such elaboration. But in fact the full implications of the existence of this kind of terrorist movement scarcely seem to be recognized. People frequently call for 'fresh political initiatives', assuming that some initiatives which would have the effect of ending the violence are available. But what kind of political initiative could disarm people set on the achievement of impossible objectives, objectives not desired by the people whom they baselessly claim to represent, and (in the case of the territorialists) passionately rejected by the majority of those inhabiting the territory whose liberation is their immediate though not their sole aim? The answer has to be that no political initiatives capable of meeting these requirements exist. These demands are in themselves not negotiable; and the problems created by them are therefore not capable of solution by political means – since the judges of whether such a solution is satisfactory have to be the only people who can voluntarily stop the violence, who are the people who are perpetrating it, and who are the authors of the impossible demands.

This situation is so painful to contemplate that people naturally have a tendency to avoid seeing it clearly. Mistaken analogies are eagerly clutched at. The fact that the same names – Sinn Fein and IRA – which belonged to those by whom the Anglo-Irish treaty of 1921 was negotiated are also used by the contemporary terrorists and their friends, is one source of confusion. If a Government could negotiate with the Sinn Fein–IRA of those days why should not a Government of today negotiate with the Sinn Fein–IRA of today? After all, if today's IRA have used violence, so did the IRA of 1921.

It seems clear that some British political leaders must have had

H.—B

some such thoughts in mind when they agreed to meet Provisional leaders in 1972 and 1973. But the analogy here, superficially so tempting – and so useful not only to Irish but to *all* revolutionary terrorists – is profoundly and perilously misleading. The vital difference between the old Sinn Fein–IRA movement and the new is not in point of the admissibility of violence in principle, nor yet in point of the character of the violence used (though there are major differences there) but quite simply in the representative authority of the old Sinn Fein, and the lack of all representative capacity of the modern Sinn Fein – or more than the lack, the specific repudiation of that movement by the very people whom it claims, in some mystical sense, to represent. The old Sinn Fein had a real claim to be a liberation movement, because it was really chosen to represent a majority of those whom it claimed to be liberating. True, it did not have a mandate for violence, nor had the elected representatives control over the violence actually used. But they had, and they retained, a genuine popular base. Modern Sinn Fein–IRA has no such base. The importance of the distinction in terms of political morality is obvious.

But there is also a vital, and somewhat less obvious, distinction in terms of practical politics, of negotiation and of 'delivering' what has been negotiated. The Sinn Fein negotiators of 1921 could accept something significantly less than what Sinn Fein had promised to get; they could accept that, not only because they knew that what Sinn Fein had promised was not obtainable, but because they knew that most of the people whom they represented were heartily sick of all the bloodshed, and would gladly settle for something significantly less than what they had so blithely voted for in 1918. Thus the negotiators had a determinant counter-weight against the absolutely predictable violent repudiation of the treaty settlement by a section of those who had fought, as they believed, for the full Sinn Fein programme. There was a bloody but short open struggle; the negotiators and their supporters won; they governed the new state until they were replaced by democratic process ten years later.

No negotiations with present-day Sinn Fein–IRA or any similar organization could conceivably lead to any equivalent, or otherwise desirable, outcome. For these men have no constituency, other than doctrinaire, fanatical gunmen like themselves. If negotiators on behalf of such a constituency were to agree to something less than the impossible objective for which they all claim to be fighting, those negotiations would have no democratic countervailing force against the inevitable and savage backlash from among their own followers. And what on earth, in any case, is there to negotiate *with*? The Provisionals for their part have nothing to offer except the cessation of violence. The violence is also their sole claim to political attention. What political object can they gain that can compensate them for voluntarily relinquishing their sole claim to attention, and for disappearing into political obscurity? Short of the millennium, it is hard to imagine any political object which can compensate for political suicide. The notion – prevalent both among some Unionists and some others – that they might be persuaded to take this course in exchange for political concessions to elected representatives of the population on whose behalf they claim to act is wholly illusory. They repudiate those representatives as firmly as those representatives repudiate them. There is in fact no political end that such a group can gain from negotiating with a democratic government, *except the prestige of being seen at the negotiation table*. And since there is no available successful outcome for the negotiations they must break down, and there is no way of reopening them except by renewal of the violence which brought them about in the first place. And the fact that negotiations have occurred raises the hopes of the terrorists, confirms them in their belief in the efficacy of their chosen methods, and encourages them to increase their intensity.

It seems to follow that the quest for a political solution to the problem of political terrorism in a democracy is not only hopeless but actually leads in the opposite direction to that intended, by increasing rather than diminishing the violence.

I am not saying that political initiatives and political developments are not desirable in the areas where terrorists are active. They may be, and they may – they will, if they are well chosen – have a *long-term* beneficial effect in relation to terror, by helping to isolate and discourage its practitioners. But it would be over-optimistic to assume that any political initiative will 'solve' terrorism, and it is particularly unwise to advertise some favoured development as being about to have that effect. For that leaves to the terrorist the power to falsify that prediction and he also has the incentive to do so, since the favoured development will necessarily fall short of the terrorist's impossible full demands.

If there is no political solution, at least in the usual sense of that term, neither is there any purely military solution. It is understandable that some people should dream of ending the cycle of terror by a series of spectacular shoot-outs on the lines favoured by certain American big-city police chiefs. But these methods, through their effects on neighbours and bystanders, add to and diversify the terror, rather than end it. There is in fact no certain way of ending it but there are more and less hopeful ways of seeking to end it. The more hopeful ways include:

Convincing the terrorist that he is not going to get his own way (that involves refusal to talk with him, since though he can argue fluently from his own peculiar premises, he is not accessible to rational argument, based on premises other than his own);

Depriving him as far as possible of the publicity he so avidly seeks (that also involves refusal to talk with him);

Refusal to be impressed, confused or diverted by the versatility of his propaganda campaigns;

Unremitting, but not unrestrained or indiscriminate, pressure by the security forces;

Support for those forces from the public.

Clearly not all these ways are fully within the control of democratic governments. Most of them involve the cooperation of the public and of the media. And there are problems about that. Some of them are specific problems confined to particular countries or areas. But those I should like to consider briefly here are those which generally affect reactions of democratic publics to terrorist conspiracies, in ways which help the conspiracies and weaken democracy.

One major factor is the sense of guilt which many educated middle-class people feel about the privileges they possess, and which of course they don't want to give up. The democratic system has done much to mitigate the effects of inequality, but shows no signs of abolishing inequality itself. So one way of distancing oneself from one's own privileges, without abdicating any of them, is to detach oneself internally from the democratic system, to pride oneself on seeing through its shams – though seeing through them to what it would be hard to say. Thus, when the terrorist strikes, he is seen as in some way striking against these shams, which are seen as upheld by 'institutionalized violence' – a very useful term from the terrorist's point of view. Those who use that term seldom pause to consider that it may be much better to institutionalize violence, within a democratic system, than to allow it to shape institutions of its own, which it entirely dominates – as in the case of the private armies. But those who use the term thereby equip themselves with a justification for neutrality between the democratic state and its armed enemies. And professional considerations often also seem to favour such neutrality. Thus, in a recent book on the Herrema kidnapping, the author (a journalist) appeared to pride himself on 'neither flattering nor condemning either side'. The two sides between whom the balance was thus held even were the armed kidnappers and the police who were trying to rescue the kidnapped man. A certain number of journalists, academics, clergymen and others seem to have a somewhat similar concept of professional detachment.

Some, without actually supporting the terrorists, go a little beyond 'neutrality', in that they sentimentalize the terrorist, seeing him as a 'dedicated' person, a 'misguided idealist'. The importance of this tendency, to which clergymen appear particularly prone, is that it encourages the illusion that the problem may be solved by meeting with the terrorist leaders, reasoning with them, mediating between them and the Government and so on. And all this, with the publicity which accompanies it all, is the very stuff on which the terrorist feeds.

The 'misguided idealist' notion rests on the fallacy-ridden assumption that, since the terrorist voluntarily runs risks, he must be morally superior to the rest of us, who run no more risks than we have to. This ignores the rather obvious fact that the power which grows out of the barrel of a gun, and the kind of glamour which surrounds that power, are to some people so attractive in themselves that they outweigh the risks involved. The terrorist leaders are people of that stamp. Their fanatical devotion to their cause, or 'ideal', provides them with a sense of righteousness in pursuing the course of action which they find most gratifying. This is a sustaining combination.

I have spoken of a kind of guilt, a kind of neutrality, and a kind of sentimentality, as among the tendencies in democratic society which encourage the terrorist as he fights against that society. These tendencies of course overlap, and all of them can sometimes be found together within the confines of one newspaper article, speech, lecture or sermon. They are often accompanied by an attitude of mind which might be identified as unilateral liberalism. This is the kind of liberalism which is sensitive exclusively to threats to liberty seen as emanating from the democratic state itself, and is curiously phlegmatic about threats to liberty from the enemies of that state.

Liberals of this sort appear to be blind to the plight of those who live in fear and under oppression, not because of some abuse of state power, but because that power does not effectively extend to their district of town or country, and because therefore much of their lives is spent under the armed and arbitrary rule of terrorists, or of so-called counter-terrorist vigilantes. Too many people in Northern Ireland today have to live under such primitive jurisdictions, or worse still in the no-man's lands between them. To those who have to live under such forms of disseminated despotism the complaints of the unilateral liberals about erosion of liberty by the state must seem strangely irrelevant to what has actually happened to *their* liberty, unmourned by those who defend liberty on one side only.

The tendencies I have mentioned are part of our democratic society, fruits of its history. They do make life easier for the terrorist, and they are consciously and eagerly exploited by his propagandists. They may also, it is true, provide a safety factor, by preventing the democratic state from over-reacting, thereby moving towards its own destruction. That claim can be made, and supported with examples from the past, not only by unilateral liberals but by liberals who are more generously endowed, geometrically speaking. There are also, however, dangers in *under*-reaction, whether against revolutionary terrorists or vigilante terrorists, as the history of the Weimar Republic reminds us. If the tendencies I have mentioned had been less strong, terrorist movements would, I think, be less protracted, because less sustained. In part, the disease carries its own remedy. The protraction and extension of terrorism weaken the tendencies that have favoured that protraction and that extension. When the booby-trapped car goes off in your own street you are that much the less inclined to dwell on the idealism of those who put it there.

The democratic version of liberty is imperfect but known. The terrorist versions combine the perfections of fantasy with the reality of arbitrary power over whatever can be covered by the barrel of that gun. However long it takes, the democratic struggle against the underground terrorist empires, whatever slogans they may use, is a struggle for real liberty for real people. I think the people understand that rather better than some of those who seek to advise and instruct them.

American Aid to Freedom-Fighters?

On the radio I heard a prominent New York politician of Irish origin explaining the killings in Northern Ireland. The Irish Republican Army was a band of freedom-fighters. The struggle was the age-old one of Ireland against Britain.

The interview was on a transatlantic line. The interviewer was an Irish girl, from the Irish national broadcasting station. She was aware that something was missing from this picture. 'What about the Protestants in Northern Ireland?' she asked.

The politician was bland. The Protestants in question were very fine hardworking people. They would, in his opinion, have a magnificent contribution to make to a United Ireland. In that case, the interviewer wanted to know, why didn't these Protestants make this contribution, by actually joining a united Ireland? The answer was simple: the British. The British were preventing the Protestants of Northern Ireland from joining a United Ireland.

Now, this particular politician is neither naïve nor ignorant of Irish realities. He knows that Ulster Protestants, by an overwhelming majority, have for generations asserted their will to remain in the United Kingdom. He knows of their deep-rooted aversion to being incorporated in a united Ireland, which in their view would be a Catholic-dominated state. He should also know of Britain's declaration at Sunningdale (1973) that Britain will not oppose the unity of Ireland, if a majority in Northern Ireland come to support that, and of the corresponding declaration by the parliament in Dublin that the unity to which the Republic aspires can only be achieved by the free consent of a majority in Northern Ireland. He certainly knows that the initial deployment of British troops, in a law-enforcement capacity in Northern Ireland in August 1969, was for the protection of Catholic minorities against Protestant majority violence, including the violence of the largely Protestant local police.

The politician's version of a complex and exceedingly dangerous reality was grossly distorted and oversimplified. But that very distortion is an important part of the reality, for it helps to keep the IRA alive and to attract recruits and above all money to its cause. Of course, the farther away from the scene you are, the more plausible and the more attractive the myth can be made to appear. It is easily and quickly grasped, and it appears to be fitted with a simple and entirely satisfactory solution: 'Brits out'. The myth demands virtually no cognitive or other intellectual effort, permits unlimited righteous indignation, and requires, on the part of people living far away from the scene, no risk and only small, occasional financial sacrifice, to be transmuted into human sacrifice 3000 miles away. The news of the result can be a thrill for which no guilt need be felt, since the blame for all the deaths, by the rules of this horribly simple game, lies at the door of the ancient enemy. The angry response of certain Irish-Americans to any attempt to discuss the realities of the question has, I think, to do not so much with love for Ireland – certainly not in the sense of loving the actual Irish who live there – as with the natural human tendency to resist any intrusion on a system of satisfying fantasies.

For the IRA itself, as well as for its American supporters, the idea of Ireland is an abstraction altogether too precious to be entrusted to the actual living people of Ireland. It is probable that no 'war of liberation' has ever been fought with so little support from the people who are supposed to be being liberated, and in the face of so much outright rejection and condemnation by that same people. In the Republic of Ireland all the democratic parties, an overwhelming majority of the parliament speaking for an overwhelming majority of the people, not merely reject and condemn the IRA but have enacted, and recently strengthened, severe repressive measures against it. In Northern Ireland the Protestant majority are of course bitterly hostile to the IRA, and some of them indiscriminately vengeful against anyone thought of as sympathizing with it. The Northern Catholics are traditionally cast as sympathizers, both by many Northern Protestants and by the propaganda of the IRA itself. This again is a highly misleading picture. It is quite true that the long-standing sense of grievance of the minority in Northern Ireland, the frustrations of second-class citizenship and persistent high unemployment, provided the IRA with favourable opportunities. It is also true that some Catholic areas in 1969–70 initially welcomed IRA individuals and units in the mistaken belief that their role would be the purely defensive one of protecting the ghettos against such attacks by Protestant mobs as occurred in August 1969 and later.

However, one of the paradoxes of that period was that the same (Catholic) people welcomed *both* the British Army *and* the newly founded Provisional IRA, as, in effect, two lines of defence against danger from the Protestant side. The IRA, for its part, saw the British Army as an enemy more 'real' (in traditional terms) than Protestant extremists (traditionally, 'misguided fellow-Irishmen'), and saw the ghettos not as places to be defended from outside violence, but as springboards for the eventual liberation of a territory. While all the people of Northern Ireland – and people in the Republic and in Britain, too – have suffered as a result of the IRA's terror campaign, the people who probably have suffered most are the people whom the IRA has been claiming to 'protect': the Catholic minority in Northern Ireland. They have suffered from sectarian reprisals organized by Protestant extremists (and answered on equivalent sectarian lines by the IRA); they have suffered from the actions of British troops in quest of the IRA and its arms in Catholic areas; and they have suffered at the hands of the IRA itself, whenever they have ventured to call for a halt to its violence, or otherwise thwarted its will.

Catholic rejection of the IRA campaign has been strongly expressed *both* by the elected representatives of that population (the SDLP), by the Catholic bishops (who rejected the folly of attempting 'to bomb a million Protestants into a United Ireland'), and most recently through the impressive mass marches of the Women for Peace movement which has presented the spectacle, unprecedented in Northern Ireland, of large numbers of women crossing the ghetto lines, uniting Catholics and Protestants together, to call for an end to all the violence, from whatever side it issues. In the Catholic areas the IRA has responded with officially disavowed intimidation (as have Protestant extremists elsewhere), but these brave women have stood their ground, and have been supported by parallel large-scale demonstrations in the Republic.

It is clear, then, that the IRA is explicitly repudiated, not merely by a large majority of the people of the island of Ireland, but by a large majority in all three of the main sections into which that population has been divided by history and tradition and their political consequences.

Nonetheless, the IRA not merely continues to exist but has been able to conduct, over more than half a decade, one of the most ferocious and sustained terrorist campaigns in history. I shall consider later some of the consequences of that campaign, and the consequences which would flow from what its organizers would consider its successful further progress. I doubt whether even they consider 'victory' – essentially, though not nominally, a united Ireland controlled by its 'liberators' – as a possibility for this generation.

'For this generation . . .' These words come very easily to the lips of traditional Irish Republicans, and the branch of the IRA now actually engaged in terrorism – the Provisional IRA – is highly traditional. The meaning of the words in an Irish Republican context is not immediately intelligible to outsiders. Yet that meaning is essential to an understanding of the IRA as an enduring phenomenon, and of the full sinister significance of helping that phenomenon to endure. It is therefore necessary to say something here both of Irish history, as Irish Republicans conceive it, and of actual Irish history, of which the Republican myth is part, but which contains other vitally important elements which the myth ignores or distorts. I know from experience that Americans are apt to be impatient with harping on the past, whether that past is real or imaginary. Very reasonably, you want to hear about the here and now, and how it is all likely to turn out. Unfortunately, in Ireland conceptions of the past are very much part of the here and now, and powerfully affect the range of future possibilities.

As a revolutionary organization, the modern IRA can trace its origins convincingly enough, back to the 1860s, to the Irish

Republican Brotherhood, remembered generally as the Fenian movement, from the name of its American wing. The significance of the word 'Republican' was that – Britain being a monarchy – it implied total separation of Ireland from Britain, with no possible compromise, whereas the constitutional nationalists, like Daniel O'Connell earlier and Parnell later, were prepared to accept less than total separation. The term, derived from the French Revolutionary period and the writings of the Irish pro-Jacobin Theobald Wolfe Tone, was intended to mark a complete break with constitutional nationalists' objectives, matching a break with their methods, since the Fenians were committed to the use of physical force, which the constitutional nationalists rejected.

Most Irish Catholics in the nineteenth century followed constitutional nationalists politically and gave almost no support to the military activities of the Fenians, but at the same time they cherished, in varying degrees, vaguely pro-Fenian sentiments. A good Fenian funeral could attract a following enormously greater than anything the living Fenian could have commanded. A Fenian *past*, including if possible a prison sentence, was often a passport to a successful future as a constitutional nationalist. Fenian ballads were extremely popular with people who, in practical political activities, supported constitutional nationalism. Constitutional leaders themselves liked to use Fenian-like rhetoric, especially about the past. Among people who formally condemned Fenian violence, it was reckoned a source of pride to have Fenian friends or relations,* while any social or family tie with an 'informer' – even if in constitutional theory a law-abiding citizen – was an undying disgrace.

Names and circumstances have vastly changed, but this inherited ambivalence – understandable enough in the earlier period – still affects contemporary attitudes towards the IRA and the law. To a remarkable degree, the contemporary IRA has appeared to be unimpressed by the enormous volume of public repudiation and condemnation directed against it in Ireland. Disapproval is ineffective if ambivalence is sensed as underlying

---

*As a boy I was much prouder of the fact that my grandfather had been a Fenian in his youth than of his having been, in his maturer years, an Irish Parliamentary Party MP. My values have changed; my age also.

it, and there has been considerable ambivalence in the language of many public men – a tendency to condemn violence but to go on to say something that helps to justify it. That ambivalence has greatly waned but has not altogether disappeared. Until it does, the IRA's lifeline to public opinion will not be severed.

While some nineteenth-century attitudes subsist, new puzzles have been added to the old ones. One of the strangest is that the modern Irish state, the Republic of Ireland, which condemns the IRA and is condemned by it, has been deemed to owe its origin to the actions of members of the Irish Republican Brotherhood from which, on grounds not easy to refute, the modern IRA claims descent. This situation creates intellectual and moral difficulties which some contemporary Irishmen find painful either to explore or to see explored by others.

It is certainly true that the Easter Rising of 1916 was planned, timed, and directed by members of the Irish Republican Brotherhood. They acted, of course, without any democratic mandate, in the name of an ideal concept of Ireland, transcending the actual views or wishes of the actual people of Ireland at any given time. The Fenians, the men of 1916, and the contemporary IRA have all in turn regarded themselves as the custodians of this ideal, and as licensed by it to take any lives which they have decided are standing in the way of its fulfilment. But although the Easter Rising was in a tradition, it gave a new twist to that tradition. This was due to the strange personality, original genius, and concentrated will of the most influential of the leaders of the rising, Patrick Pearse.

The Republican movement, during the nineteenth century, had been generally known as 'the physical force movement'. It had thought, often wildly enough, in terms of imminent success, and it had repeatedly failed. For most Irish people – and for Irish schoolchildren to this day – there is something depressing about the contemplation of all these failures. Pearse, on the other hand, felt exaltation at the thought, not exactly of failure, but of the continual renewal of blood sacrifice for Ireland. Pearse was, of course, by no means unique in the exaltation of his romantic nationalism. This was a prevalent mood throughout Europe before and during the First World War. In Ireland it was quite a natural response to contemporary English jingoism. What was special about Pearse was the intensity of his commitment to a sacrificial form of nationalism, his vision of the past as a long chain of sacrifices, and his imaginative understanding of the power over the future which further sacrifices could exert. He was determined himself to be part of such a blood sacrifice, inspiring other blood sacrifices, as the Fenians had done. No man better understood the power of funerals; it was at the funeral of the Fenian dynamiter O'Donovan Rossa that Pearse spoke the words most often quoted by the contemporary IRA: 'And while Ireland holds these [Fenian] graves Ireland unfree shall never be at peace.' The concepts of the divine and of recurrent Irish blood sacrifices were fused. The Proclamation of the Republic in Easter 1916 begins with the words: 'In the name of God and of the dead generations . . .' W. B. Yeats, himself an occasional, fickle, but all too memorable propagator of the sacrificial cult, summarized the lesson:

> For Patrick Pearse had said
> That in every generation
> Must Ireland's blood be shed.

Now, the leaders of the contemporary IRA are not like Patrick Pearse in temperament, character, or methods. They are not mystics or poets, or chivalrous dreamers, nor are they drawn to self-immolation. Pearse would have viewed with horror their version of the re-enactment of the sacrifice: their bombings of restaurants and pubs; their murders of civilians in their houses; their knee-cappings and tarrings and featherings; their sectarian reprisals; their intimidation and extortion. The Proclamation of 1916 specifically repudiated 'inhumanity' and 'rapine' as well as 'cowardice'. Nonetheless Pearse's interpretation of history is important in two ways to these his unforeseen and gruesome disciples. First of all, just as they are insulated against democratic repudiation by the whole élitist Fenian tradition, so they are insulated against failure by Pearse's interpretation of history. Thus they are not perturbed if it can be shown both that their bloody actions are repudiated by almost the entire community, and that they are doomed to failure. Within the tradition to which they belong, their personal importance is that they are renewing the blood sacrifice 'in this generation'. If that sacrifice does not result in freedom now, then that will be the fault not of the tiny fighting minority, but of the majority which is – as in the past – unworthy of them.

The Irish Republican movement, or condition, is thus distinguished from other revolutionary movements in being *failure-proof*. Its greatest blunders are successes if they produce more martyrs, the guarantors of ultimate victory, in however remote an epoch.

Normal learning is by trial and error, and error is eliminated by examining the causes of failure. The Irish Republican condition, being incapable of failure, is also incapable of learning. Derived from a culture which has for long placed little value on rationality – a word which Irish printers almost automatically misprint as the more familiar term *nationality* – Irish Republicanism prides itself on reiteration, in thought, word, and deed. It is an infinitely dreary system, of desolating durability.

The 'Republicanism' I am discussing here is both the traditional and the dominant form of militant Irish Republicanism, the ideological driving force of the Provisional IRA. I am not concerned with the 'progressive' and 'Marxist' versions of Republicanism, extant in the so-called Official IRA, which for a while competed with the Provisional IRA in terrorism and then gave up the struggle. There would be plenty to be said about them also, but it seems more urgent to talk about the form of Republicanism for which men are now killing people, and collecting money for that purpose in America. The Officials were never good at reaching Irish-American money; their Marxist language stood between them and potential subscribers. The more traditional Provisionals have been much more successful here. However, their 'policy documents' do not adequately reflect their archaic ideology. Such documents are compiled by intellectuals, more or less, and use language intended to sound modern and thoughtful, about federal structures, community government, a nine-county Ulster, and the Lord knows what. People who read this stuff about theoretical democratic forms may not be aware that it is produced on behalf of an authoritarian military organization which in practice rejects and despises all democratic process.

But anyone who has seen a Provisional rally, and listened to what gets the cheers, knows that 'community government' and similar gimmicks are not what this is all about. It is about blood.

The system I have described is inherently proof against reasoned argument, but its proponents can themselves effectively refute arguments which claim to derive from, or be consistent with, the non-rational assumptions from which the IRA itself derives its mystique and continuity. This is the second way in which an image of the 1916 rising continues to be of service to the contemporary IRA.

The *tactics* of the contemporary IRA can certainly not be justified by Pearse's *example*. But the *concept* of the IRA – the renewal of the bloody conflict until the connection with England is altogether broken for all Ireland – is fully in line with Pearse's *doctrine*. And Pearse's doctrine was long accorded, and to a lesser extent still is accorded, a quasi-sacred status in nationalist Ireland. The state, of which Pearse is rather paradoxically regarded as a founder, has been quite successful, pragmatically, in containing the IRA. But it has been less successful ideologically, in so far as its nominal ideology has derived from the same sources as have sustained, and do sustain, the organization which it seeks to suppress. At the level of the crossroads pub – and at higher levels too – few people have been able to refute the arguments of the local Republican, because these arguments are generally based on or closely related to assumptions which have been, and to some extent still are, widely prevalent in the culture. This has especially been so when the local Republican talks about liberating the six occupied counties of Northern Ireland. The Irish nationalist tradition generally – and not just in its Republican or extreme forms – has always tended to over-emphasize Britain's responsibility for partition and to ignore, or gloss over as irrelevant, the fact that a majority of the people in Northern Ireland do not want a united Ireland. It is only fairly recently that the implications of this reality have begun to sink in, as far as the population of the Republic is concerned.

Another long-established convention of political rhetoric and official history holds that the Irish state derives its existence from the Easter Rising, and implies that, without that rising, the British would still be in occupation of all Ireland. Formally, the IRA does not accept this conventional doctrine – since, in its view, the existence of a twenty-six-county state is a betrayal of the Easter Rising. Informally, however, the IRA has derived great benefit from the implications of the doctrine. After all, if the gun got us the degree of freedom we have, why not let the gun finish the job? The argument can have a powerful appeal, especially to minds sufficiently unsophisticated, or uninformed, to have accepted it at face value in the first place. Most potential recruits to the IRA possess such minds.

The relation of the Easter Rising to the present Irish state is of course much more complex and ambiguous than the conventional doctrine seeks to assert. Up to a point, the Easter Rising was a spectacular triumph of failure, exactly in the line of Pearse's thought.* The British wartime government, as if working to Pearse's script, saw to the consummation of the blood sacrifice, through sixteen executions, in circumstances which seemed designed to produce, and did, the maximum revulsion against the British, as well as an emotional swing in favour of the dead men and their surviving comrades, and against the hitherto dominant constitutional nationalists. This revulsion – combining with other factors of less relevance to our subject – led to the overwhelming victory of Sinn Fein (the heirs of 1916) throughout nationalist (Catholic) Ireland in the general election of 1918. (The Protestants of Ulster continued to vote Unionist as before.) In Irish Republican retrospect this electoral result constituted not only an endorsement of the rising, but also an irrevocable mandate to renew an armed struggle for freedom. In fact, the people had not been asked for such a mandate. Sinn Fein, in its electoral campaign, had taken great care to avoid any suggestion that support for it meant support for an armed struggle. The people were encouraged to think that Sinn Fein, refusing to sit in the British parliament, would state the case for an all-Ireland sovereign state to the peace conference, and that the case would be irresistible, given the Wilsonian commitment to self-determination and the freedom of small nationalities.

These hopes were, of course, doomed to be disappointed.

*See Ruth Dudley Edwards, *Patrick Pearse, The Triumph of Failure* (Gollancz, London, 1977).

What followed in reality was guerrilla war, and the counter-guerrilla terror of the Black and Tans. Finally, in 1921, the British offered a settlement. This settlement contained significant improvements over the version of home rule which had been offered to the constitutional nationalists before the war and before the guerrilla, but it did not differ *in kind* from that earlier offer. The main political case of the heirs of 1916 against the constitutional nationalists was that the latter had – most reluctantly – agreed to the partition of the island. But the same heirs – some sooner and some later – eventually had to accept basically the same thing.

The present Irish state was established not in 1916 or in absolute terms, but in 1921 on the basis of a compromise. The limited self-government (for twenty-six counties) obtained in 1921 was to develop into sovereign independence for the same area. I see absolutely no reason to suppose that the more limited self-government offered to the constitutional nationalists could not equally well have developed into sovereign independence for the same area, without the need for any violent uprising.

I am not here arguing a 'violence achieves nothing' case. In this situation, among the things it ensured was further violence, in an indefinite perspective and in accordance with Pearse's uncanny vision. The new violence began immediately, with the Irish Civil War of 1922–3, between those who accepted the Anglo-Irish treaty of 1921 and those who rejected it. It flared up again briefly at intervals, over the decades thereafter, but the present politico-sectarian strife in Northern Ireland has already cost more lives than what we still call 'the Civil War', and has lasted longer than any previous 'war' in Ireland since the seventeenth century.

'Ireland unfree shall never be at peace . . .'
So when will Ireland be free, and at peace?
The Republican answer is: 'When Britain stops interfering in Ireland.' Today, the main emphasis is on the withdrawal of British troops from Northern Ireland. I shall examine in a moment the question of whether such a withdrawal would leave Ireland at peace or not. But would withdrawal even leave Ireland free in Republican terms? I think it would not. On the most

optimistic – and in my view least realistic – assessment of what would happen then, there would have to be an agreement involving the elected representatives of Ulster Protestants, Ulster Catholics, and the Dublin Government on forms of institutions for Northern Ireland. This is not at all what the IRA want. To them *all* these groups of Irish people – although between them they represent all the people of the island – are already guilty, in varying degrees and ways, of collaboration with Britain. Any agreement between them would therefore be automatically denounced as having been rigged by Britain. In such conditions Britain would not have *really* withdrawn from Ireland: she would be continuing her interference through her stooges, dupes, and so on. Ireland would still be unfree, and could not therefore be left at peace. In the Republican tradition the judges of whether Ireland is free or not are of course not the people of Ireland, nor their elected representatives of all shades, but the pure minority of committed Republicans, 'the faithful few'. Even if some Republicans were to accept such a settlement, those who refused – whether in a minority or not – would be the pure, licensed, to continue the struggle. If the sole arbiter of what constitutes freedom is the IRA, then freedom can only be interpreted as absolute victory for the IRA – not merely over Britain, but also over all sections of the Irish people. As long as this kind of Republican tradition exists at all, Ireland will continue to be 'unfree', and the custodians of the tradition will thereby have a permanent licence to kill.

The ideological reasons for the persistence of the IRA are strong, but they are not the only reasons. The conventional British Tory picture of the IRA as 'thugs and gangsters' leaves out an important reality: the fanatical and apparently impenetrable conviction which Republicans have about the justice of their case, the legitimacy of their own actions, and their moral superiority over those who condemn them. Their ideological armour, strange and archaic though it may appear to others, is of immense importance to their morale and their durability. 'Thugs and gangsters' won't do, though there are plenty of those around, but 'dedicated idealists' doesn't cover it all either. There are risks and hardships attaching to IRA membership, but there are also benefits. Members of the IRA, from the ordinary 'volunteer' up to the leaders, enjoy a certain prestige as long as their organization is actually killing people, and their movement also depends on that for funds. Violence can become addictive, and so can the power over others which it confers. The campaign has now lasted long enough to develop vested interests of its own, reinforcing the inbuilt ideological commitment to persistence even in conditions which are utterly hopeless.

I have considered the prospects, even if British withdrawal under IRA pressure could conceivably be followed by political agreement between the representatives of the two communities in Northern Ireland, and with Dublin. An agreement between these parties might be possible – and I hope some day will be possible – *if the IRA were to disappear from the scene*. But if the IRA were still active, and if British withdrawal appeared in the light of a surrender to it, then no such agreement would be possible, and what would be likely to follow would be sectarian civil war on a Lebanese scale. A certain Ulster loyalist tradition is quite as bloody-minded and fanatical as that of the IRA, and its adherents are vastly more numerous, especially in the most densely populated parts of Northern Ireland. I have no doubt that if the British were to withdraw in such circumstances these loyalists – with massive Protestant support – would move to 'deal with the IRA once and for all' and in doing so would show little mercy to the population which they regard as having given aid and comfort to the IRA: the Catholic minority in Northern Ireland. I have no wish here to speculate about the dimensions or exact nature of this catastrophe, or about its political consequences in the Republic of Ireland, in Britain and elsewhere. But one thing is certain: it would *not* lead to a united Ireland. Its consequences could include a new border in a new place; they would certainly include – after many dead, many injured, many refugees – a deeper and more bitter division between the two communities in Ireland.

The reader may be inclined to dismiss this picture as just a personal nightmare. There are some people, by no means all of them Republican apologists, who dismiss such fears as exaggerated or capable of being exorcized by reassuring language about *'phased withdrawal'*, as though the rate of the process would transform the nature of its consequences. An announcement of intent to carry out a phased withdrawal of the troops would in fact be likely to precipitate a feverish build-up of 'defensive capability' in both communities, leading toward civil war quite as surely as plain withdrawal would do. The consequences of withdrawal are widely recognized, even among people whom one might assume to be committed to this 'solution'. I know a British MP who was once attracted to the 'troops out' movement. Meeting him in 1973, I noticed that he had changed his opinion and I asked why. He said it had come about as a result of more visits to Northern Ireland, and of one experience in particular. This was a meeting with a deputation of Long Kesh dependents – wives and mothers of then interned Republicans. Towards the end of the meeting, the MP put the simple question: 'What do you think would happen if we pulled the troops out?' The answer was memorable: 'We'd all be murdered.' He had the impression that the feeling was general.

This was the feeling of women whose menfolk *wanted* the British troops out and, at least in some cases, had been trying to drive them out by force. It also followed the very worst period in relations between the troops in question and the Catholic population: the period (1971–2) of the use of interrogation techniques subsequently condemned by the European Commission on Human Rights, and of the 'Bloody Sunday' shooting of thirteen unarmed men in Derry. In reaction to IRA violence, directed at them out of Catholic areas, British troops had tended to treat Catholics generally as hostile, and the British Government of the time had not discouraged the tendency, as subsequent British Governments (both Tory and Labour) have done. In these circumstances the MP knew that women like these hated the British troops. What shook him was the genuine dread, even in this quarter, of what would happen if their own menfolk 'won' and the hated troops actually went.

The answer, though it was blurted out by a 'Republican dependent', was not a proper Republican answer. In terms of IRA strategy, the kind of catastrophe I have very lightly sketched is an acceptable price for the success which the withdrawal of the troops would represent. 'Civilian casualties', as one of their leaders has said, 'are inevitable in urban guerrilla warfare.' Even the fact – in so far as the more intelligent among them recognize it – that the consequences of withdrawal would leave Ireland still partitioned, is not a deterrent. 'What if unity is not achieved in this generation? There will be plenty of other generations.' What is important is that 'this generation' will have struck its blow, and sacrificed its blood; and the consequences of withdrawal would certainly include the greatest blood sacrifice that Ireland has seen since the bloody insurrections of 1798 and their still bloodier suppression. It is true that, after this slaughter, Northern Ireland, whatever the extent of its territory, would have no place for the IRA; the Catholic ghettos would be gone, in one way or another. As against that, conditions *in the Republic* would be much more propitious than ever before from an IRA point of view. The influx of refugees, the legacy of indignation and bitterness, the inflammation of nationalist passion, would all nourish Republicanism and prepare the way for the 'final struggle'. By this time, the Northern Protestants would no longer be 'misguided fellow-Irishmen' – indeed, that term is already somewhat out of fashion – but 'Britain's garrison in Ireland', to be crushed or driven out. In the meantime the liquidation of 'traitors' in the Republic itself could proceed.

These prospects are not openly contemplated by the IRA at present. Its propaganda likes to paint a rosy picture of peace by agreement (implicitly between the IRA and its Protestant enemies) after a planned and phased British withdrawal. But the actions of the IRA do not point towards any such result, and its directing brains must know the probable consequences of any 'success' these actions could conceivably win. The basic case against the IRA is not that its methods are horrible, though they are that. The basic case is that the only kind of 'success' that these methods can win is even far more horrible in human terms than the present methods themselves; and that a movement which can use such methods towards such successes, is anti-human.

I don't believe the IRA is likely to 'succeed' in this way, although that dark possibility does remain. Yet I also find it hard to believe that the IRA will speedily fade away. To what extent the great public repudiation of it, especially by the Northern Catholic women, will affect its operations remains to be seen. There are signs that it is aware that it has a serious problem here, and that it is not sure how to cope with it. A similar, more limited peace protest by women, led the other IRA – the left-leaning Officials – to call off their terror campaign in 1972. The Provisional IRA is, however, more fanatical and traditional, more abstract in its attitudes, and is not, like the Officials, theoretically committed to winning mass support. ('What mass support did the men of 1916 have?')

I believe that in the long run the durability of the IRA depends on the durability of the special political culture that has nurtured it. To the extent that public men continue to pay lip service to assumptions for which IRA men risk their lives, then the IRA has an advantage and a recruiting ground. There is, as I have indicated, a growing impatience with that kind of lip service, a growing sense of what it can cost.* One hears less about unity being 'the first national aim', even from lips accustomed to shaping such syllables. There is – there has had to be – more thinking about people, and less about nationalist abstractions. In the Republic, the traditional emotional weapons of the IRA – such as the exploitation of hunger strikes, funerals, etc. – have in recent years notably failed in their traditional effect. These conditions have not stopped the IRA, but they may inhibit its development.

Straightforward disgust with the IRA and all its works has greatly increased, and the traditional ambivalence has correspondingly decreased. Considerable traces of it are however still discernible, more I suspect among 'opinion-formers' in the media and elsewhere than among the general public. Anyone who attacks this ambivalence is liable to be accused of being unpatriotic. The accusation is founded on the assumption that patriotism implies loyalty to traditional attitudes, without regard to the inadequacies of these or their contemporary cost to human beings.

As far as Northern Ireland is concerned, the 'British troops out' people have an apparently attractive solution, while those of us who oppose them may appear to be advocating that these troops remain there forever. Neither the Irish nor the British want that. There is now quite general agreement that the people of Northern Ireland should be encouraged to work out their own

---

*An over-optimistic reflection. In the General Election of 1977 the voters gave Fianna Fáil, the party which provides most of the lip service in question, a massive majority.

affairs by accommodation between the two communities. Unfortunately, a stable basis for such an accommodation has not yet been found, despite repeated efforts and the brief apparent success of the Sunningdale agreement, shattered in 1974 by the joint effects of a continued IRA offensive and loyalist industrial action, combined with intimidation. The unexpected successes of the peace women may conceivably bring into being a basis for future, more stable, accommodation, through the exercise of effective community pressure on the killers in both communities. If that pressure succeeds, the killings stop, and stable accommodation then takes place, Northern Ireland can police itself under agreed institutions, and the troops can safely go. But failing that, the troops cannot safely be withdrawn.

The IRA campaign is at present a main factor in keeping the British troops in Northern Ireland, as well as in poisoning the relationship of the two communities there – not uniting Ireland but dividing it even more deeply. Those, in America and elsewhere, who are contributing to this campaign are contributing to those effects, to the protraction and possible escalation of human suffering and to no conceivable other result of benefit to anyone except the fanatics who collect the money and do the killing.

Theorists of Terror (One)

Mr Bowyer Bell opens his *On Revolt: Strategies of National Liberation* with a chapter on 'The Nature of Revolt'. The theoretical base of his analysis is shaky. On the very first page we are told that 'Antigone denied authority and the gods'. This statement is a certificate of unfitness to write about the nature of revolt. The whole point of Antigone is her *refusal* to deny the gods, even when ordered to do so, on pain of death, by local and temporal authority. And the whole point about the tradition of revolt which she represents is this assertion of a higher law and loyalty, as against the rulers of a particular place at a particular time. In the case of revolts of national liberation – which take us away a bit from Antigone – the gods are both ancestral and somehow identified with the order of the universe. The Irish Republic, on Easter Monday 1916, was proclaimed 'in the name of God and of the dead generations from which she [Ireland] receives her old traditions of nationhood. . . .' The leaders of other 'revolts of national liberation' may use a different style – the higher laws invoked may not be those of History – but the principle is the same. Revolt has to be in the name of something higher than that which is revolted against. Rebels are unusually pious people; always in what they profess, and quite often in reality. Not entirely a compliment: pious people can also be cruel and devious,

New York Review of Books, 16 September 1976. The books under review are: J. Bowyer Bell, *On Revolt: Strategies of National Liberation* (Harvard University Press, 1976); J. Bowyer Bell, *Transnational Terror* (Am. Enterprise Inst. for Public Policy Res., 1975); Edward Hyams, *Terrorists and Terrorism* (St Martin's, New York, 1975); Sam C. Sarkesian (Ed.), *Revolutionary Guerrilla Warfare*, (Precedent Pub., New York, 1975); H. Jon Rosenbaum and Peter C. Sederburg (Eds.), *Vigilante Politics* (University of Pennsylvania Press, 1975).

for the higher good. In the Judaeo-Hellenic tradition the proto-
types are Antigone, in one branch, and the Pharisees (with a
significant difference), in the other. It makes no more sense to
have Antigone deny the gods of Thebes than it would to have the
Jewish rebels against King Herod revolt at the same time against
Jehovah.

The frivolity implicit in Mr Bell's approach to Antigone is
evident also in the structure of his new book. The revolts he
considers are all revolts *against Britain*, yet he makes the claim that
'broader conclusions' can be drawn from a range of examples
thus specifically limited:

These rebels against the crown – seven very different movements
motivated by the most diverse ambitions – applied a remarkably wide
spectrum, however defined, against an equally remarkably consistent
opponent. This existence of a single British stage, the twilight empire,
permits a greater degree of comparative analysis than might a different
mix of case studies, but it by no means limits the results to an isolated
sub-genre. The revolts against the crown were special, but not so
special that broader conclusions are merely speculative. . . .

Instead of a simple series of isolated, independent case studies of
anticolonial revolts, where rebels succeed or fail in the mountains or
in the back alleys, what evolves from the postwar generation, tentatively if not clearly, is an anatomy of revolt that can with some profit
be compared to other rebels.

That last horrible sentence is the conclusion of the chapter on
'The Nature of Revolt'. The confusion of the language matches a
confusion of ideas. The only valid conclusions one can draw from
examining case histories of revolts against Britain are limited to
revolts against a power of that kind. Even there, the seven cases
considered do not include India, where revolt took many forms.
They do include one case (Ghana) that was hardly a revolt at all,
and one (Malaya) whose course and outcome were quite unlike
the others, probably because it was not seen as *just* a revolt against
Britain, but as part of a Communist attack on 'the free world'.
Studies of 'revolts of national liberation' directed against one
declining power are not likely to shed much light on the course
or prospects of revolts against powers which have not declined.
Perhaps they are not intended to.

Mr Bell develops the concept of 'strategies', given prominence in his title, in his opening chapter where he discusses various national 'models' with capital letters: Optimum Moment, Instant Alternative, Alternative Legitimacy, Incremental Strategy, Magic Means. When he gets down to his case histories, however, he has little or nothing to say of these strategic fancies – though new ones such as the 'Strategy of the Stationary Epicenter' pop up occasionally – and in his concluding essay he comes near to abandoning the idea of strategy altogether. He acknowledges that the rebel's 'strategy' is often 'little more than the mix of possible tactics under an appropriate ideological banner'.

'All things seem to limit the rebel's options, to restrict his strategy to tactics, his organization, cause, scenarios and expectations limit his prospects.' Quite so. A recent article on Marion Coyle, one of the kidnappers of the Dutch businessman Herrema in Ireland, gives a whiff of the reality:

The Irish Republicanism in which she was more and more absorbed was an intensely tactical affair. There was nothing intellectual about it. A person who shared a cell with her during her first period of imprisonment says: 'even inside we never discussed *why* we were doing it.'*

Mr Bell's treatment of his case histories, when he gets down to them, is much more sensible and straightforward than one might think likely from his generalities and excursions into theory. His seven case histories are: Palestine, the Gold Coast (Ghana), Malaya, Kenya, the Suez Canal Zone, Cyprus and South Arabia (Aden). He also considers Northern Ireland, as a sort of afterthought; he is the author of a useful, though now dated, book on the IRA. The best of his individual studies is that on Palestine; his exploration of the relations between the Irgun and 'official' Zionism is of great interest, notably for the account of 'the Season', the Haganah's campaign against the Irgun and the Stern Group, an episode 'forgotten' – as Mr Bell points out – in conventional retrospects of the period.

During 'the Season', which lasted roughly from October 1944 to July 1945, it was the policy of the Haganah – to summarize Mr Bell's account – to cooperate with the British forces in combating terrorist activities, felt to endanger Zionist postwar objectives,

*Eamonn McCann, 'The Marion Coyle Story', in *Sunday World* (Dublin), 25 April 1976.

especially after the murder of Lord Moyne in November 1944. This policy broke down when the Zionist leadership reached the conclusion that these objectives would not, after all, be attained by negotiation. It is doubtful how far the Zionist leadership realized the long-term consequences of setting – or accepting the setting of – an example of 'the effectiveness of terrorism' in the Middle East conditions. Certainly the competing terrorists of that region have made good propaganda use of that example, in all the borderlands of Israel, including ruined Lebanon. (Similar, though not identical, considerations apply to the Irish guerrilla of 1919–21, the cult of that guerrilla, and the rise of the Provisional IRA.)

Mr Bell's study of South Arabia is also very interesting, and one aspect of what 'national liberation' can mean emerges particularly clearly from it. This aspect concerns not the 'foreign oppressor' – who is on his way out anyway – but the question of who is to rule the territory when he is gone. This was the *sole* question really involved in the fighting in South Arabia, but it has also been present, more subtly, in other 'national liberations'. Nkrumah's mass demonstrations in the Gold Coast, ostensibly directed against the British, really defeated the old African élite of the Gold Coast itself, and replaced it by the new élite of Nkrumah and his friends. Recourse to arms in Ireland in the 1916–22 period had similar effects. Self-government (for what is now the Republic) was coming anyway; what the violence determined was not the departure of the British, but the question of who should be in charge after they left. Violence can indeed achieve results, but the results are not necessarily the same as those which its beneficiaries claim for it.

Mr Bell's very short book *Transnational Terror* deals mainly with fairly recent international acts of terrorism and concludes with what looks like an appeal for a moderate response:

These new transnational terrorists may be countered with special techniques, technological innovation, the deployment of new knowledge, the enactment of new law, or by quiet diplomacy and discreet coercion, but hopefully not by recourse to counter-terror or means alien to traditional American sensibility. And perhaps where possible real efforts can be made to alleviate the legitimate grievances that fuel rebel frustrations. Most important, the threatened must accept that however spectacular the deeds of terror, they are more easily tolerated than prevented.

'Hopefully', perhaps where possible and perhaps not. Mr Bowyer Bell, like Machiavelli, sees that terrorism can have its uses. He does not rule it out for 'our side', and finds the general public too squeamish on the subject:

Sometimes the public finds terror unacceptable even when it is the more merciful alternative. Few of the uninvolved want to be told that the judicious murder of scores of Vietnamese headmen might be a more effective and humane technique for controlling the countryside than the indiscriminate use of B-52s. In America, after the trauma of the last decade, few can view assassination dispassionately as a merciful means to effect change in areas where conventional politics might engender more widespread violence.

Mr Bowyer Bell writes about terrorists with a degree of sympathy which the present reviewer, being perhaps oversensitive on the subject, finds moderately repugnant. He sometimes, though not consistently, adopts the language of the terrorists themselves, terming their killings 'executions' or, even worse, using coy euphemisms like 'elimination', and he is impressed by the 'logic' or 'elegance' of various bloody deeds. He thinks that 'the practitioners of terror can largely be categorized on the basis of their aspirations' and resists other methods of categorizing them, such as those which would include, among others, the categories of lunatics and gangsters. He thinks that psychotics can 'mimic revolutionary violence', while criminals 'may drift on the violent edge of revolution', but 'the true terrorist' is something else. He does, however, admit that 'tidy academic categories readily become blurred when applied to real-life situations'. One is reminded at this point that he has, after all, met real-life terrorists in Northern Ireland.

Edward Hyams, the author of *Terrorists and Terrorism*, is one of those pacifist anarchists who are so hostile to the 'institutional violence' of even democratic states that they end up with a relative justification of non-governmental terrorism. He insists, repetitively, that terrorism is 'effective', which is true in so far as it produces effects, most tangibly in the form of dead people. Like Mr Bell, but much more unwarily, he is disposed to be snobbish about that difficult distinction between terrorists and those other 'victims of institutionalized violence', the ordinary criminals. Thus he rebukes George Woodcock for calling Nechayev 'this sinister youth'. 'Even granted that Nechayev was a murderer and a blackmailer, he was so in his self-made *persona* as a dedicated terrorist; he was certainly not a common criminal.' But no one said he was a common criminal; fortunately he was a most uncommon one. It is possible to think of most 'common criminals' as *less* sinister than those rare murderers and blackmailers who are also 'dedicated'. One would also like to know, and not just from their own lips, exactly what each of them is dedicated *to* – that *why?* which the imprisoned Marion Coyle would not discuss. As a harassed vigilante told a contributor to *Vigilante Politics*: 'the line between dedication and screwballs is very close.'

Mr Hyams gives Ireland much space, but little attention. 'Since the freedom of Ireland and the establishment of the Republic were won by terrorism, the Irish case deserves two chapters to itself.' Bully for us. There were indeed – and are – terrorists in Ireland, of various types, and there are various views of their 'effectiveness', and what and whom it has served. But the odd thing about the particular terrorists whom Mr Hyams believes to have won the freedom of Ireland is that they weren't there at all:

By 1912 the Irish terrorists had convinced even that part of the British Establishment which had thrown out earlier Home Rule Bills, of what Irish Parliamentarians and publicists had not been able to convince them and probably never would have convinced them, that the Irish must be given Home Rule.

But in 1912 there were *no* Irish terrorists active, either in Ireland or in Britain. The last terrorist campaign – and a singularly ineffective one – had been nearly twenty years before, in the mid-1880s. The Home Rule Bill of 1912 was the product not of terror but of parliamentary pressure, with the Irish Party holding the balance of power in the British Parliament. The terrorists of several sorts came later, much later, with a world war in between. Mr Hyams's version is notable for the strength of the wish behind it: he wants so much to see terrorism as the key to historic change that he simply infers from the change itself that it must have been preceded by terrorism. As he says later, 'There is no point whatever in trying to blink away the truth . . . Let us take a long, hard look at the facts.'

Mr Hyams also writes about Palestine and about czarist Russia. Having tried him in an area I know something about I am not prepared to accept him as a guide in other areas. In a penultimate chapter he comes back to Ireland again, with undiminished conviction of the success of terrorism: 'It is terrorism, not argument, that is responsible for the project to create a Council of Ireland; and if that is not a step towards union of all Ireland, I don't know what is.'

'The project to create a Council of Ireland' in 1973–4 can be seen as a terrorist success; if so it was a success of the kind that was immediately cancelled by another success, for the Council of Ireland succumbed – a good many months before Mr Hyams's book was published in New York – to a combination of continued terrorism by the IRA and industrial action (backed by vigilante-type intimidation) from organized Protestant loyalists in Northern Ireland. One of the reasons for the strong loyalist reaction was that loyalists believed, with Mr Hyams, that the project for a Council was both a victory for terrorism and a step towards a united Ireland. To the degree that a given result is ascribed to terrorism it will be regarded as vulnerable to counter-terror; especially where the terrorists are a minority of a minority, as in Northern Ireland.

Revolutionary Guerrilla Warfare is a bulky anthology of miscellaneous writings on this subject. Most of the essays (reprinted from various periodicals) are by contemporary American academics, but there are also selections from Sun Tzu and Mao Tse-tung, summaries of Clausewitz and Che Guevara, Lenin's 1906 paper on partisan warfare, and the text of Carlos Marighela's famous and fatuous *Minimanual of the Urban Guerrilla*. The academic contributions range from general theory – one essay has the appetizing title 'The J.-Curve of Rising and Declining Satisfactions as a Cause of Some Great Revolutions and a Contained Rebellion' – to micro-studies like 'Political Mobilization in Guinea–Bissau'.

Most of these studies were written at various dates between 1968 and 1972, and they often bear the marks of their period. One

essay entitled 'An Approach to Future Wars of National Liberation' (1971) by Avrom H. Katz (of the Rand Corporation) is
in fact an attempt at an approach to what is now a *past* war – that
in Vietnam. For Mr Katz, Vietnam was an 'interdisciplinary war',
to be won by setting up an interdisciplinary agency.

This essay is a museum specimen of a once-prevalent form of
academic 'contribution' to the war effort, and on that ground
perhaps might merit inclusion in a 1975 anthology. But I do not
have the impression that that was the reason for its inclusion. The
editor seems to take all his contributors equally seriously, and must
be a very confused man. The last essay in the book (other than a
note on 'sources') has the title 'Morality and National Liberation
Wars' (1971). The author, Professor Charles Burton Marshall,
equates morality with what he calls 'prudence', and 'prudence'
with a refusal to allow 'allocations for strategic security' to be
encroached on by 'great social programs'.

Vigilante Politics is by far the best and the most disturbing of the
five books under review. It has a clearly defined subject: the use
of illegal violence in support of an established social and political
order, 'order without law'. The individual essays, almost all of
which were written specifically for inclusion in this book, are all
of high quality and together make a coherent whole, in three
parts.

Part 1 is theory; Part 2 is about vigilantism in the United
States, and Part 3 contains examples from Asia, Africa, and
Europe. Anyone at all inclined to make the fairly common
contemporary assumption that illegal political violence is mainly
a left-wing affair will have to think again, if he or she even looks
at the impressive evidence which accumulates in this volume
about the persistent recurrence of right-wing illegal violence,
throughout the world, over a long period. Vigilantism, say the
editors in their introduction, 'consists of acts or threats of coercion
in violation of the formal boundaries of an established socio-
political order which, however, are intended by the violators to
defend that order against some form of subversion'.

Among the ways in which subversive violence can be 'effective'
is the unleashing of vigilante violence, as in the case of Northern
Ireland (discussed in this volume by Richard Ned Lebow).
Right-wing violence, like the left-wing kind, attracts the

commoner varieties of criminals: 'Quasi-criminal elements are attracted to the movement as a semi-legitimate avenue for the expression of their anti-social tendencies'. In their relation to Northern Ireland, Protestant criminals are 'vigilantes', while Catholic ones are 'subversives'; the other way round would not even be 'semi-legitimate' in the relevant eyes.

The recent rise in vigilantism in the United States, and the extent to which it is condoned by the press and the media, are no doubt among the reasons why the editors set about making this valuable collection, and the part of the collection which deals with contemporary vigilantism in the United States is both impressive and disturbing. The key essay here is 'Community Police Patrols and Vigilantism' by Gary T. Marx and Dane Archer. The authors of this pioneering essay have gathered 'descriptive information on twenty-eight self-defense groups . . . based on interviews with police and patrol group members, observation, newspaper accounts and analysis of documents'. They break down the groups studied into four categories, defined with a shrewd eye for relevance, in relation to the attitude of the police:

Type 1: Supplemental and encouraged by police.
Type 2: Supplemental and opposed by police.
Type 3: Adversarial and encouraged by police.
Type 4: Adversarial and opposed by police.

Only the first two categories are strictly vigilante, in relation to the society generally, but the last two are vigilante in relation to their own communities, while all four share the 'self-defence' psychology of vigilantism. (Of course a body can be *both* subversive *and* vigilante: thus the IRA is subversive in relation to Northern Ireland and the United Kingdom, but has a vigilante aspect inside the Catholic ghetto.) The authors note a tremendous increase in the number of privately owned handguns – from ten million to forty million in ten years – and a very high level of support for citizen anti-crime patrols: in the Boston region 55 per cent of whites and 69 per cent of blacks supported these patrols. The authors put the two sides of the case:

Who, after all, can be opposed to self-defense? In the best of American violent and populist traditions, the groups can be seen to represent
H.—C

action and involvement, self-help, embattled neighbors banding together in a righteous crusade against the dark forces of crime and disorder. Yet there is clearly another side; the antidemocratic potential of privately organized citizen violence. Mass enthusiasm for direct action in the face of institutional restraints (the law, courts, elected officials, formal police bureaucracy, and procedure, etc.) for many people raises the spectre of the Ku Klux Klan and European fascist groups. The picture of independent armed entrepreneurs patrolling 'their' heterogeneous communities is not one that can be unequivocally welcomed.

They note that if the Boston levels of support for citizen patrols were typical of urban areas the number of Americans who would support such patrols would be over 42 million. They go on to say:

These perhaps unexpectedly high levels of support for citizen patrols make it interesting to speculate about the potential for vastly more widespread citizen mobilization in America under various forms of provocation. For example, if crime or riots and social movements were more sustained or perceived as more of a threat than they have so far been, and law-enforcement authorities were unable to restore order, would literally millions of Americans pick up the gun to respond to the perceived threats with private violence?

Understandably, they don't answer this question. They do however conclude that citizen patrols are going to be a lasting feature of American city life:

To judge from the last ten years and the conditions of the cities, more responsible and sensitive regular police are not likely to be forthcoming in adequate supply. In such a context we may be left with the patrols as the better of limited alternatives.

The citizen patrols are of course on the borders of legality: they have potential for counter-terror but, perhaps with some exceptions, are not now engaged in it.

The book is full of bracing insights. For example this, on educating policemen:

There is no proof that education makes people any kinder or more law abiding. There is some proof that it makes people smarter. Smarter policemen will not automatically eschew vigilantism as a tactic or practice. As a matter of fact, there is good logic in saying that the increased education may help the policeman have the requisite perceptual talents to be a true vigilante (rather than an ordinary brute).*

In the space available to me I cannot give anything like an adequate description of the observations and ideas in this collection. Frightening though much of its content is, it is refreshing to see so much intelligence now brought to bear on one significant part of the generally murky field known as 'conflict studies'.

Not long ago, I contributed to a symposium on British television on political violence. I argued that there was no justification for political violence *in a democracy*, no justification for ambiguity about such violence, or failure to support its repression under law. What I said was, I believe, right in its context. But in generalizing about democracy I left out of account an important distinction which is made in the essay by Marx and Archer on vigilante politics:

Max Weber has argued that a major characteristic of the modern state is its ability to claim 'the monopoly of the legitimate use of physical force within a given territory'. But compared to highly centralized European countries, this process is much less pronounced in the United States, a country whose Bill of Rights guarantees each citizen 'the right to bear and keep arms'. Where it exists the struggle between citizen patrol groups and the state is part of a broader historical process and the unresolved conflict over the role of force in modern American life.

If democracy includes placing 'the monopoly of the legitimate use of force' under the control of elected representatives, as generally in Western Europe, then a clear distinction can be drawn between the legitimate democratic monopoly and *all* illegitimate competition. In America, the distinction cannot be drawn in just that way. Violence, both potential and actual, is too diffuse and too sanctioned, and tolerance for vigilantism – including police vigilantism – too widespread for the tidy 'European' distinction to be tenable. Democratic process can be used to pay for illegal violence, as recent revelations about the FBI and CIA have shown.

The Church committee report on Intelligence Activities has raised (without fully answering) the question: 'What happened

*'Vigilantism and the American Police', by Kanti C. Kotecha and James L. Walker.

to turn a law enforcement agency [the FBI] into a law violator?' The violations included incitement to violence as the report also shows: 'Although the claimed purpose of the Bureau's COIN-TELPRO tactics [inside the United States] was to prevent violence, some of the FBI's tactics against the [Black Panthers] were clearly intended to foster violence and many others could reasonably have been expected to cause violence.' This is the kind of tactic which is partly deprecated and partly condoned in the passage from Mr Bell's book quoted above, and the most obvious gap in *Vigilante Politics* is its silence about such activities (that collection was certainly planned, and most of the essays presumably completed, before the recent spate of revelations).

Mr Bell's opinion that by murdering a few people you may save the lives of a lot more, is obviously not confined to Mr Bell. But in fact there is no calculus of violence permitting such certainties, and the often rather dim minds which experiment in this area have no real conception – as the documents published by the Church committee make amply clear – of what forces they may be playing with or what they may let loose. The tendency to see 'international Communism' as the arch-enemy can blind people to more elemental forces, and an apparently clever anti-Communist stroke can unleash violence on a much greater scale than would have been likely without such a stroke.

Thus, in Ireland, certain members of Mr Lynch's Government in 1969–70 encouraged the toppling of the then 'Marxist' leadership of the IRA and the establishment of a new IRA led by 'good Catholics': the Provisionals. But in fact, in this particular situation, the 'Marxist' leadership had been a factor tending on the whole to *confine* violence, in the conditions of Northern Ireland. It sought indeed to promote class war, but to avoid sectarian civil war. And in Northern Ireland it is sectarian issues, not class issues, which are explosive. The 'good Catholics' who replaced the 'Marxists' dismissed the danger of sectarian civil war as 'unreal' and now find themselves engaged in precisely such a struggle.

The bloody cycle of sectarian–political retaliatory murder has attained its present intensity as a result not only of the forces of terrorism and vigilantism, but also of the efforts by elected persons (in 1969–70) to manipulate forces which they failed to understand. I do not know whether the Irish political Sorcerer's Apprentices who conjured up the Provisionals had any international mentors, but they certainly had models. When democratic governments, whose strength and appeal are in the rule of law, break that rule, they are inflicting a real and certain damage on themselves and those whom they represent, in exchange for a purely hypothetical gain, which may in fact turn out to be a supplementary damage.

The forms of the danger vary, as between America and Europe. The American system, with its guarantee of 'the right to bear arms', may be more democratic than most European systems, but it is much more violent. (Northern Ireland is extraordinarily violent by European standards, but by American standards what is extraordinary about it is not the level of violence but the ways in which violence is legitimized.) Americans have, on the whole, rather more cause than Europeans* to put to themselves Yeats's question:

> What if the Church and the State
> Are the mob that howls at the door?

There would be wide agreement that, for people living under military despotisms, or subjected to other forms of government in which they have no say, the right to rebel exists. Only despots or pacifists would be likely to deny this. The assertion of a right to use political violence in a democracy is a different matter. Such a right can be asserted against the denial of minority rights; or it can be justified on the grounds that democratic processes are fraudulent. Certainly minority rights have been violated in democracies, and certainly democratic processes can involve a good deal of fraud. Yet it does not seem to me that either of these truths can be plausibly invoked to justify major or sustained political violence in a democracy. The cause of minority rights may be and probably has been served by episodes of token protest, blackmail, violence, but sustained political violence would be suicidal, almost by definition, for any minority population. *Vigilante Politics* is full of grim instruction in that matter. The Catholics of Northern Ireland know by now some of the cost of being protected by terrorists.

*If this sounds like European complacency I can only plead that the thought was suggested by a corrective comment by two American scholars, quoted above, on a generalization by a European, Max Weber.

As for the fraudulency, what is in doubt are not the frauds of democracy, but the claim of the terrorist groups to be replacing fraud with truth. Their own organizations are authoritarian-militarist, tending towards a monopoly of both fraud and power. The career of Joseph Stalin, from the 'dedicated' terrorist in Baku to Lord of Gulag Archipelago, is relevant here. It is true that apologists for the terrorists can make effective use of the point that the democratic politician's condemnation of terrorist violence is hypocritical, since the democratic state is violent itself. But in so far as this charge rests on the concept of 'institutionalized violence' *under law*, it is not very convincing. Where the use of violence can be restricted and restrained, under the rule of law, there is an advance in civilization, from which terrorism is a regression.

But of course wherever democratic leaders themselves sanction illegal violence they have no effective moral response to the terrorists, because they are terrorists themselves. The various types of terrorism and vigilantism, accelerating by reciprocity, are capable of destroying democracy. No one who reads *Vigilante Politics* will be likely to feel that threat as remote or unreal, or to doubt that if democracy perishes in an advanced industrial country a form of right-wing authoritarianism, resembling fascism, will take its place. The glorification of the terrorist/vigilante, whether it comes from the right or the left, is a pro-fascist phenomenon in societies like those in North America or Western Europe.

If we go back to the sources of our civilization, we find that Antigone rejected not law, but authority that failed to respect the law; this rebel was no terrorist. As for the Pharisees, they were terrorists all right, and brought ruin on the society whose values they set out to defend. Christ's preference for the publicans remains relevant, as Simone Weil saw.

Theorists of Terror (Two)

These books are part of a rapidly growing literature about the use of violence for political ends, or ostensibly for political ends. Both books range widely in time and space, and they overlap to a considerable extent. There may be a conceptual distinction between terrorist and guerrilla – though I confess it still eludes me after reading these two volumes – but in practice the two are so often found to be mixed up that any conceptual distinction between them becomes blurred. This does not worry Mr Parry who – as you might infer from his title – tends to see terrorism as the use of violence by people he doesn't like – an attitude with which I sympathize emotionally but must deprecate intellectually. Dr Laqueur's approach is more academic and – though this does not necessarily follow – his book is much the more valuable of the two. Yet he too fails to establish a clear and stable distinction between guerrilla and terrorism, or to confine himself, in terms of his announced distinction, to his announced subject. He deprecates the term 'urban guerrilla' and makes the valid point that it is used for propaganda purposes, to avoid the pejorative connotations of the words 'terrorist' and 'terrorism'. Yet the grounds on which he would deny validity to the term 'urban guerrilla' seem to me not very firm. 'The essence of guerrilla warfare', says Dr Laqueur in his preface, 'lies in the fact that the guerrilla can hide in the countryside and this, quite self-evidently, is impossible to do in a city.'

One has to agree that a gunman – however one chooses to

New York Times Book Review, 23 January 1977. The books under review are: Albert Parry, *Terrorism: From Robespierre to Arafat* (Vanguard, New York, 1976); Walter Laqueur, *Guerrilla: A Historical and Critical Study* (Little, Brown, Boston, 1976; Weidenfeld and Nicolson, London, 1977).

denominate him – cannot 'hide in the countryside' in the city. But he can and does hide in the city. Both in the city and in the country, gunmen can hide, emerge to kill and destroy, and go into hiding again. It is not at all self-evident that different names have to be applied to this pattern of activity, according as it is practised in the city or in the country. By that criterion – applied to the Irish situation – the same IRA gunman, when hiding in South Armagh, would be a guerrilla warrior, but when hiding in Andersonstown, Belfast, would be a mere terrorist.

It is true that Dr Laqueur also posits a distinction based on scale, which could rather more safely be maintained: 'There have been guerrilla units of ten thousand men and women but an urban terrorist unit seldom, if ever, comprises more than a few people, and urban terrorist movements rarely consist of more than a few hundred members.' Yet this distinction is also imperfect. Urban guerrilla/terrorist activities are carried out by small groups, but many *rural* guerrilla/terrorist activities have also been carried out by small groups, including one of the most successful of all in modern times – Castro in the Sierra Maestra. If smallness makes the terrorist, these are rural terrorists.

The truth is that these are not purely analytical terms, and cannot be made to work as such. They are heavily charged by the history of past human attitudes to violence, their use is conditioned by our own political judgements about particular uses of violence in the present, and by feelings affecting such judgements, and affected by them. By immemorial tradition *war* is legitimate violence. Guerrilla – little war – 'guerrilla warfare' implies at least a degree of legitimacy: belligerent status may be round the corner. 'Terror', 'terrorism', 'terrorist' – isolating the element of fear which all violence must inspire – necessarily evoke all our negative feelings about violence, and place at a distance the calming concept of legitimacy.

Also, for English-speaking persons interested in discussing such topics, guerrilla has that halo of distance: romantic figures in foreign countries, engaged in some vaguely perceived opera of violence, evoke quite different feelings than are wrung from you by the spectacle of your neighbours' legs, arms and heads being collected in plastic containers outside the bombed-out shell of your local supermarket. In this perspective 'urban terrorism' is indeed very different from 'guerrilla warfare'. Country people who have actually experienced the rural guerrilla might not agree, but do not greatly influence published comment. The nearer the violence, the less likely it is to be seen as legitimate. Compare the degrees of support for the IRA among Irish-Americans, and among Irish people actually living in Ireland.

The concept of legitimacy dictates the selection of examples in Mr Parry's large and sprawling book, although the author nowhere clearly articulates such a concept. Why for example begin with Robespierre? Terror as an instrument of government is as old as government itself, and the terror of 1793 is by no means the bloodiest in recorded history. The reasons why that terror can be seen as *the* terror, and why a writer like Mr Parry finds it natural to begin there, do not derive directly from a moral revulsion from political violence, but from the political judgement that *revolutionary* violence is illegitimate, and from the tendency to restrict the application of the alarming word 'terror' to violence seen as wholly illegitimate. Similarly it is natural for Mr Parry to exclude all acts committed in the course of war between sovereign states from the otherwise very wide scope of his survey of terrorism. An anarchist's bomb killing five or six people ranks as terrorism but Hiroshima does not. The reason is not that Hiroshima was less terrible, or less intended to terrify, but that its terror is seen as legitimate, and that legitimate terror is not called by that name.

I do not want to be taken as implying that the concept of legitimacy is irrelevant, or that there is no such thing as legitimate use of force: only a thoroughgoing pacifist – who has necessarily also to be a thoroughgoing anarchist – could make such assertions. What I object to about Mr Parry's approach is not the fact that he applies concepts of legitimacy, and reflects them in his vocabulary, but that he shows no awareness that this is what he is doing, or that there are difficult problems involved in the relations between authority and violence.

Both books reviewed here often make fatiguing and depressing reading, because of the great accumulation of violent case histories which they contain. In the case of *Guerrilla* the accumulation is drawn from an even longer span of time than in *Terrorism*, because Dr Laqueur begins his examples in classical times. But

Dr Laqueur, unlike Mr Parry, does a great deal more than accumulate examples; he reasons about these, and draws significant inferences from them. The concluding part of his book – Chapters 8, 'Guerrilla Doctrine Today', and 9, 'A Summing Up' – is particularly important and deserves to be read by all who are seriously concerned with the problems of violence in modern society. He believes, rightly I think, that the strength and potential of guerrilla movements have been exaggerated mainly as a result of the successes and ostensible successes of these movements in the decolonization period when the people they were fighting often wanted to get out anyway. In this last part of the book he seems to lose sight – to his own advantage – of the distinction he sought to establish earlier between guerrilla and terrorism. In one of the most striking passages in the book he shows how the apparent helplessness of democracies in dealing with terrorism can be deceptive:

Democratic regimes always seem highly vulnerable to terrorist attack. The constitutional restraints in these regimes make it difficult to combat terrorism and such failure exposes democratic governments to ridicule and contempt. If, on the other hand, they adopt stringent measures they are charged with oppression, and the violation of basic human rights. If terrorists are put on trial they will try to disrupt legal procedure and to make fair administration of justice impossible. Having been sentenced, terrorists and their sympathizers could then claim that they are victims of gross injustice. Up to this point, the media (always inclined to give wide publicity to acts of violence), are the terrorists' natural ally. But as terrorists' operations become more frequent, as insecurity spreads and as wide sections of the population are adversely affected, there is a growing demand for tougher action by the Government even if this should involve occasional (or systematic) infringements of human rights. The swing in popular opinion is reflected in the media focusing no longer on the courage and unselfishness of the terrorists but on the psychopathological sources of terrorism and the criminal element – sometimes marginal, at others quite prominent, but always present in 'urban guerrilla' operations. Unless the moral fiber of the regime is in a state of advanced decay, and the political will paralyzed, the urban terrorist will fail to make headway beyond the stage of provocation, in which, according to plan, public opinion should have been won over to their cause, but is in fact antagonized.

I think that in seeing the media as generally 'reflecting' – rather than shaping – public opinion, Dr Laqueur is right. In my opinion they tend to reflect it with a considerable time-lag, especially where political violence is concerned. But the whole question of the relation of the media to political violence on the one hand, and to democracy on the other, deserves to be the subject of a separate and detailed study. Dr Laqueur might be the right person to undertake it. If he does I can promise him a rich vein of material in Ireland, North and South.

Political Violence

I have recently been reading a number of academic studies of this subject and related themes – terrorism, guerrilla war, vigilantism, etc. – and I have been struck by the clinical detachment of the tone of several of these studies. The writers appear to take a stand of something like neutrality between a democratic state and its armed internal enemies. It would be inappropriate on my part to affect such a detachment. I am committed, both by personal conviction and by responsibilities which I share, to the concept that armed conspiracies against a democratic state threaten us with a reversion to barbarism, and that the democratic state has a duty of defending civilization against these conspiracies by all means short of those which would themselves involve a descent into barbarism.

I am deliberately confining myself to the consideration of political violence *in democratic conditions*, because I believe that is the aspect of the matter which most concerns both you and me. I also think it rather pointless to discuss whether people living, say, under a military dictatorship – which is in itself a form of armed conspiracy – should or should not set up another armed conspiracy in order to overthrow the ruling one. Everything there would depend on one's guess as to the human costs involved, and to the likelihood of the new conspiracy being an improvement on the old one. The defence of democracy is another matter and permits, I think, of firmer judgement.

When I speak of the defence of democracy, I am not of course in any way defending those colonial wars which have been waged by democracies in conditions where democracy is for home

Lecture on Granada TV on 15 February 1976.

consumption, not for export. The Vietnam war, for example, was a negation, not an assertion, of democratic values. But even while that war continued, the existence of democracy in America itself continued to be of positive value and made possible the protest movement against the war, which eventually helped to end it.

I would agree, of course, that the defence of the democratic state against terrorists involves a certain kind of political violence – violence, that is to say, used in defence of a political system against people attempting to substitute for that, by violence, another system. I would prefer myself to follow the old usage whereby violence used by the state is described as force, and the more pejorative term reserved for the activities of the enemies of the state. But I am not inclined to quibble about the word and I agree that gunshot remains gunshot with whatever abstraction it may be covered.

The complete pacifist must of course reject the violence of the state, as well as that of its enemies, external and internal. This is a religious position: it is also an anarchist position. This would be wholly admirable if human beings had reached a stage where they could live in peace together without imposed restraints. This is not now the case nor does it seem at all likely to be attained even in the next hundred years. In these conditions the disarming of the state would lead to its dissolution, to the distribution of power among groups prepared to use violence, and probably to external intervention – all of which would entail greater violence than follows from the normal retention of the law-enforcing apparatus of the state. A convinced religious pacifist would be prepared to accept even these consequences, but ordinary people would not.

It is true, of course, that even democratic and welfare states and their legal structures maintain and defend institutions and practices which involve very substantial inequalities both of rewards and opportunities. Since the state is prepared to defend these inequalities by force if necessary, the whole system is often characterized as one of institutionalized violence. As a description this has a certain limited validity. Institutionalized violence is a necessary part of *every* organized state since without its availability any state would disintegrate. But those who make most use of the term tend to ignore the fact that the institutionalization of violence within a democratic system is the most responsible way available to us for containing violence. Democratic institutions can be altered by non-violent means; the use of violence by the democratic state is subject to scrutiny and criticism, and abuses can be punished and corrected. None of this works perfectly, but it works to some extent, and no such restrictions at all apply to other uses of violence, whether by non-democratic states or by terrorist organizations.

Those who make most use of the term 'institutionalized violence' often seem to suggest both that its existence justifies non-institutional violence – that is, terrorism – and that the violence of the terrorist is calculated to bring about conditions in which institutionalized violence no longer exists. I know of no evidence corroborating this hypothesis and of some impressive evidence invalidating it: both Stalin and Hitler used terror to gain control over vastly greater terror. If people prepared to use violence to get their way actually *do* get their way, there is absolutely no reason to suppose that they will not be prepared to go on using violence to see that they go on getting their way. Thus if the democratic state is overthrown the institutionalized violence will continue: what will have disappeared will be the democratic system and its safeguards.

In some left-wing commentary on current forms of terrorism we can see a romantic presumption in favour of the terrorist. Since he is prepared to risk his own life, as well as to take the lives of others, he is taken to be exceptionally unselfish, setting his cause above his own personal interests. This presumption tends in turn to generate vaguely favourable notions about the merits of the cause in question, but in fact the presumption itself is un-warranted. All we know with certainty about the terrorist are what he does and what he says. What he does is kill people, what he says is that he is killing to attain certain political ends, but there is no reason why we should take what he says on trust. He may be working for some political end, or he may be working under a political flag for essentially personal ends. The life of a terrorist, risky as it is, has its rewards. These include power – the power that grows out of the barrel of a gun – a certain kind of glamour and prestige, money, and freedom from normal routines and constraints. For some personalities this combination may be attrac-tive enough to make them want to continue their terrorist activity even if they know their ostensible political objectives to be unattainable. But of course if these objectives are really thought of as attainable, there is also an attractive *future* role for the terrorist, as in the case of Stalin and Hitler.

These imputed motivations are largely speculative but certainly no more speculative, and I think considerably more probable, than the notion that terrorists are exceptionally unselfish, or to use a favourite word of their admirers, 'dedicated'. Dedicated to what?

The only unusual thing we know with certainty about the terrorist – the thing that marks him out from other people – is his unusual propensity to frighten, hurt and kill people. This in itself is no guarantee of selflessness: some people *like* killing, frightening and hurting people and also like the other more or less tangible rewards which derive from the capacity to frighten, hurt and kill. I would therefore argue that presumptions in favour of the terrorist are superfluous and that it is more reasonable to look at him, as most people do, as a menace to society which it is important to suppress. The romantic concept of the terrorist, besides being unjustified, is an obstacle to his suppression, and that is why it is important to challenge this concept.

It is the nature of democracy, and in part a source of its strength, that it allows far freer range to its enemies than does any other system of government. The terrorist naturally takes full advantage of this, and in particular derives sustenance from his peculiar relation to the media. Violence is news: the greater the atrocity the greater the publicity. For terrorists working in these conditions, the publicity is an essential part of the game. To many, it is intensely enjoyable for its own sake but it also serves practical purposes. It helps with fund-raising: the Provisional IRA campaign could probably not have lasted this long without the money which the publicizing of its exploits has drawn from North America. The publicity also both attracts recruits and tends to spread in the community generally an atmosphere of fear which may often be helpful to terrorist operations.

The security forces, the police with the army in reserve, are of course in the front line in the struggle against anti-democratic terrorism. Victory in that struggle depends on the degree to which the society at large sees the terrorist clearly as the enemy, and on the number of people who are prepared to run at least some degree of risk to combat terrorism. These factors vary in different conditions. In my own country, Ireland, for example, a prevalent romantic interpretation of history long favoured recruitment for the IRA. To challenge that interpretation of history was therefore a significant part of the struggle against the IRA and some progress has been made in that respect.

The responsibility of the media in this area is an extremely complex subject. On the one hand it is quite certain that the terrorists do consciously use the freedoms of the media in their attempt to destroy the type of state which alone makes those freedoms possible. At the same time it has been claimed, by a Brazilian theorist of terrorism, that one of the objects of the terrorist is to force the democratic state itself to curb these and other freedoms and make itself so unattractive that the cause favoured by the terrorist eventually seems preferable. The Brazilian theory is, I think, pushed to fanciful lengths but the problem of having to defend democracy by limiting some of its freedoms is a real one. To ask the media for voluntary restraint is probably futile. The freedom of the press includes the freedom to be sensational and in a market economy sensational treatment of violence always finds ready buyers. It is probably, though not certainly, better to live with this than to attempt to curb it, except in the area of broadcasting where a degree of state regulation is necessarily involved.

The best way for a democracy to deal with what is called political violence is to set aside its supposedly political character and concentrate on its criminal aspect as an armed conspiracy. This implies a stolid refusal to do any deal with the conspirators, to concede any of their demands or to have any contact with them at all, other than those contacts that may be necessary for their apprehension and suppression and the protection of those whom they threaten. It may be argued that the foundation of the Irish state, of whose Government I am a member, provides a notable example to the contrary effect, since that state may be said to have been founded through a deal with IRA terrorists. This argument ignores the fact that the men with whom Lloyd George negotiated in 1921 had a democratic mandate from a great majority of the population of the new state – not a mandate for violence but a mandate to negotiate.

No group of terrorists at present operating in these islands has any democratic mandate at all. Any deal with any of them would be simple capitulation to the naked violence of small unrepresentative groups. In these conditions well-meaning mediators should be discouraged; mediation brings the terrorist prestige and encouragement, relief from pressure and time to regroup; for the democratic state – unless it is prepared to abdicate altogether – it can bring only a lull followed by a savage resumption of terror. There is ultimately no way of beating the terrorist except by convincing him, and above all his friends and financial supporters, that he has no chance at all of getting his own way. This may take a long time, and may involve more suffering and death, but it can and must be done to avoid the far worse consequences which follow if a democracy flinches before the terrorist threat.

State Terrorism: The Calculus of Pain, of Peace and of Prestige

> They tell you, Sir, that your dignity is tied to it [coercion of the American colonists]. I know not how it happens, but this dignity of yours is a terrible encumbrance to you; for it has of late been ever at war with your interests, your equity and every idea of your policy. Show the thing you contend for to be reason; show it to be common sense; show it to be the means of attaining some useful end; and then I am content to allow it what dignity you please. But what dignity is derived from the perseverance in absurdity, is more than I could ever discern.
>
> EDWARD BURKE, Speech on American Taxation, 1774

On 11 October 1967 the *New York Times* reported that Secretary of Defense McNamara had informed the Senate Preparedness Investigation Sub-Committee that he did not think that the bombing of North Vietnam 'has in any significant way affected their war-making capability'.

He also said that the bombing had not seriously deterred the flow of men and materials from North to South and he added that 'all of the evidence so far is that we have not been able to destroy a sufficient quantity of war material in North Vietnam to limit the activity in the South below the present level and I do not know that we can in the future' and that there was no 'direct relationship' between the level of bombing in the North and the United States forces required in the South.

The Secretary of Defense – whatever he may have said in private – gave the public no intelligible reason for persisting in a policy, that of bombing the North, which he admitted to be

---

Preface to John Gerassi, *North Vietnam* (New York, 1967).

militarily unrewarding. 'On balance', he said, 'we believe it helps us.' As the 'best evidence' for this proposition he adduced 'Hanoi's strenuous and vigorous propaganda campaign to force us to stop it'.

His basic argument in favour of the bombing policy, according to the *New York Times*, was that the bombing was having the political effect 'of increasing the price' North Vietnam 'was paying for its aggression in South Vietnam'.

The American public should know exactly what this price is and how and by whom it is being paid. Mr Gerassi's book contains some first-hand information as well as some documents about this. A part of 'the price' was paid, for example, by the child whom Mr Gerassi saw in Hanoi's General Surgical Hospital who 'had been struck by a pellet in one temple, exiting through the other, blowing out both eyeballs in the process; the child was technically alive, although of course blind and incurably deranged'.

From the type of weapons which are being used against the North Vietnamese and the conditions in which they are being used, as reported by observers like Mr Harrison Salisbury and Mr Gerassi, and from Mr McNamara's statement, it becomes evident that the fate of this child is not a by-product of military necessity but is an intended result, satisfactory to those who make policy in Washington. It is one among many thousands of similar items in the price which the North Vietnamese are to be made to pay for, in the language of Washington, their aggression in South Vietnam, or, in their own language, for resisting American aggression.

The man who holds principal responsibility, under the President for this policy, has now indicated that it does not serve any military purpose. What purpose then does it serve?

The most respectable-looking answer which has been attempted to this question – though it is one in which Mr McNamara himself does not seem to have much faith – is that the continuation of the bombing will bring Hanoi to the conference table – that is to say, will bring it in sight of accepting United States terms. The policy-makers in Washington and their specialist advisers – who are paid to consider all possibilities and evaluate them in the light of the known preferences of their superiors – have certainly considered the possibility that the bombing will have no effect at all on Hanoi's policy, and also the possibility that it will stiffen the determination of Hanoi and the North Vietnamese people to continue their struggle against a foe whose arrogance and cruelty they are given daily additional reasons to hate.

There is not the slightest evidence that the bombing policy which has been in operation since February 1965 has produced, or is likely to produce, any weakening in Hanoi's determination to carry on the struggle and it is now admitted that it has not significantly weakened Hanoi's capacity to carry on this struggle. Yet the terror-bombing continues. Why?

If a reason which was both avowable and plausible could be produced, the policy-makers in Washington have both the motive and the opportunity to bring this reason home to the public. As they have not done so, we must conclude that the motive is either not avowable or not plausible or neither avowable nor plausible.

We are necessarily driven to speculation as to what the motives covered by these descriptions may be.

We do know the general outlines of the situation in which the decision to continue the bombing is being maintained. President Johnson cannot find a way of bringing the war to a successful conclusion and he will not accept responsibility for an unsuccessful conclusion. Withdrawal from Vietnam would therefore be intolerable. It would supposedly mean a loss of prestige to the United States; it would certainly mean admitting that Johnson has been the most unsuccessful President in the history of the United States. The argument from prestige has similarly weighed with many governments in the past, including that of George III in relation to the rebellious American colonies. On that occasion the argument from prestige was definitively refuted by Edmund Burke in the passage quoted at the beginning of this Introduction. President Johnson and his advisers have not shown the thing they contend for to be reason, or common sense, or the means of attaining any useful end and they continue to derive such dignity as they can from perseverance in absurdity.

Men in power who feel that their dignity is menaced are dangerous men. In the absence of avowable and plausible explanations for the bombing policy, we cannot overlook the possibility that 'the price' which the children of North Vietnam are being made to pay is a price for the wounds which their rulers have inflicted on the self-esteem of President Johnson, Secretary McNamara and the Joint Chiefs of Staff. To judge by Mr McNamara's language, the principle behind the bombings is primarily one of punishment, that is to say, of revenge; the primitive idea of exacting a price for an offence.

Presumably there are also some calculations involved. Some members of the military establishment are known to favour more extreme and ruthless forms of offensive, possibly rising to the use of nuclear weapons and war with China. President Johnson and his civilian advisers are still apparently sane enough not to want to be carried all the way in that direction. At the same time, as Mr Roger Hilsman made clear, in his recent book, *To Move a Nation*, the Joint Chiefs of Staffs can command enough domestic political power to make it difficult for even such a President as Kennedy to risk a confrontation with them. In trying to avoid such a confrontation, Mr McNamara accordingly agrees to continue the bombing of North Vietnam, while rejecting the military arguments on which that policy was supposed to be based. As he made clear, it is a political decision, but not perhaps political in quite the sense in which he meant it to be understood. It is a policy both agreeable to the feelings of those in power and convenient for them in political terms in the domestic context.

It can even be plausibly defended, in the domestic context, *in terms of the preservation of peace*. After all, if Mr McNamara's consent to the bombing of North Vietnam, while serving no military purpose, yet enables him to withstand military pressures for even greater escalations of the war, is Mr McNamara not really serving the cause of peace by continuing the bombing – and even by escalating it, at a pace slower than the military chiefs, without Mr McNamara, would exact? And are not those who support the Administration – conscious of its brave, subterranean struggle against the Generals – wiser in their service to peace, ultimately more compassionate, and more intelligent in their compassion, than those who adopt the easy way out of calling for peace, through withdrawal from Vietnam? Nay more, even if peace were attainable, it might prove to be a trap. A recent writer in *The New Republic* who describes himself as 'bitterly critical of the war', and even as preferring NLF victory in Vietnam to continuance of the war, nonetheless dreads the consequences of peace. On certain assumptions about the future of the New Left – assumptions which he seems to regard as probably valid – he thinks it likely that 'power will go by default to conservatives and reactionaries', and adds:

This seems especially likely if the US fails to suppress the South Vietnamese revolution and withdraws. Any such about-face in Vietnam could produce a right-wing reaction even stronger than the one produced by the collapse of Nationalist China and the stalemate in Korea. . . . America may be headed for an era of repression which will make McCarthyism seem relatively innocuous. [Christopher Jenks, 'Limits of the New Left' in *The New Republic*, 21 October 1967.]

In America, then, both peace-minded people and liberals may be shown arguments to persuade them that McNamara's 'price' – payable by people in Vietnam – is worth paying. New questions enter the calculations. How many Vietnamese children and others is it necessary to kill now, and in the near future, to strengthen McNamara's hand against the Chiefs of Staff, and prevent more rapid escalation? How many Vietnamese children and others is it necessary to kill in order to preserve a relatively liberal climate of opinion in America?

Again, precise answers would be hard to attain, but it is obvious that the relevant calculations are going on, in more acceptably formulated ways:

> Behind each liberal, peace-loving eye
> The private massacres are taking place.*

It does not much matter that the evidential base for such reasoning is dubious. We have not been given serious reason to believe that if the President and Mr McNamara decided to stop the bombing, members of the military establishment could nonetheless force a more serious escalation. Nor has it been proved that going to war for Nationalist China would have produced a more amiable domestic climate than 'losing China' actually did. As regards Korea, the conclusion of peace – under a

*After Mr Auden.

Republican President – seems to have led to an abatement, rather than an intensification, of the fury of domestic reaction. Nonetheless, arguments tending to support the view that the Administration's policy on Vietnam is preferable to some terrifying if vague alternative carry some weight with a public which is already frightened and which has much to lose. The child whom Mr Gerassi saw in the Hanoi General Surgical Hospital may after all be helping to keep an American professor in his job.

Admittedly the policy, while convenient in Washington, and capable of being suitably presented to many sections of the American public, looks unrewarding in Vietnam. Yet there is, after all, the possibility, however faint, that the bombing, if persevered in and appropriately, though cautiously, intensified, may in time produce some desirable result from Washington's point of view. And even if it should produce no significant and desirable local results – as is admitted to be probable – at least the price which the North Vietnamese will have been made to pay may serve to deter those who in other parts of the world may be tempted to engage in courses liable to be classified by the United States Government as 'aggression', or in other ways running counter to United States policy and interests, or those of a President and his military advisers.

These gains are remote and doubtful. Yet since they are gains for United States policy, and in United States prestige, in the terms in which the Government may itself derive reflected prestige from them, they far out weighthe actual physical sufferings of living and dying men, women and children in Vietnam. The Vietnamese, who are being sacrificed, are external to the American political process and can only be indirectly apprehended within it, through the effects on sections of the American public of the cost of inflicting on the Vietnamese the required degree of suffering.

The calculations required here are necessarily of a complex character, and even then inconclusive. If one could establish that the killing of x thousand Vietnamese children would result in raising or lowering President Johnson's popularity on the polls by one per cent, then the problem would be simple indeed. But in practice the position is much more complex. The reduction of the terror-bombing would swing the political influence of the Joint

Chiefs of Staff against the President and thereby reduce his popularity rating; on the other hand, the reports of the bombings, the American casualties in carrying them out and the general cost in American lives and welfare in sustaining the whole policy and in amplifying it, rule out any easy assumption that there can be a predictable positive or negative co-relation between the number of deaths of Vietnamese and the President's popularity rating.

Towards this calculus of pain, of peace and of prestige, elaborate equipment is available in Washington for the collection and analysis of data. But the data are of such a nature that, however elaborate the equipment, their evaluation will still largely depend on the pressures of the situation and on the subjectivity of the evaluators.

Among the pressures of the situation is the fact that the President is known to be set on a certain course and only wants to hear such evaluations as suggest that this course, modified only within certain narrow limits, would, or at least could, lead to success. In this situation the most sophisticated position papers can be of little more scientific value than, say, the predictions of Hitler's astrologers. This is not, however, to say that the existence of such calculations – even if, as may well be the case, they are never really understood or even considered by those who make the decisions at the top – are without meaning or without importance. They are important in convincing the men in power themselves – and others – that their activity has, or could be found to have, a rational base and that it could be proved to be capable of being pressed to a successful conclusion or at least to the avoidance of a disastrous one. They seem to be important – in Mr McNamara's case if not President Johnson's – in spreading a veil of abstract cerebration between the men responsible and the concrete reality of what they are perpetrating. They are important finally and perhaps mainly for theoretical validation, for conveying to the American public the impression that their rulers are possessed, through mysterious channels, of ineffable certitudes which can be contested only by those who are ignorant of vital facts, which the Government, for reasons of security, cannot release. For the public, those banks of computers take the place of the numinous equipment of ancient shrines in providing unutterable, and therefore unanswerable, confirmation of the otherwise obscure and often silly statements of the custodians of the equipment.

As regards the subjective aspects, the character of the remaining advisers whose advice is to any great extent heard must have been to a great extent conditioned, through a sort of natural selection, by the pressures of the situation. It is known that many of the Kennedy advisers have dropped away and at least one of them – Mr Roger Hilsman – has subsequently indicated that the reason for his dropping away was his knowledge that President Johnson was determined to win military victory in Vietnam. Granted the nature and history of the war, the adviser who remains, or who emerges, to be heard advising in such conditions must be of a rather special kind. I suspect, perhaps wrongly, that the type of mentality, or psychology, which is likely to be drawn to nuclear games theory may be liable also to find it congenial to think about the exact price which it will be most profitable to make Vietnamese people pay for their Government's persistence on a course which United States policy has decided to present as aggression. A man who enjoys thinking about himself thinking about the unthinkable has already cast himself in a particular role which may inflect his advice.* If you are accustomed to thinking in terms of how many tens of millions of deaths and maimings among *American* civilians constitute an acceptable price for some political action, then the vicarious and hypothetical stoicism thus acquired will be helpful – in terms of such reasoning – to you in the practical business of calculating the amount of terror which can most profitably be applied to the Vietnamese population. When men come to regard the making of such calculations as proof that the calculator is on a superior intellectual plane to the mushy-minded

---

*I do not here refer specifically to the author of the well-known book *Thinking About the Unthinkable*; my comment is on a class of men whom I conceive to be touched by the intellectual hubris reflected in his title. My friend and colleague Mr Peter Nettl, with whom I have discussed this, considers, on the other hand, that the influence of the games theorists is most likely to be exerted *against* the present Vietnam involvement. This may well be true of them as a class. My point here, however, is that the type of calculator whose calculations are likely to ascend to a relatively high level in the *present* decision-making process – granted the President's known predilections – is likely to be covered by the description in the text. And any calculations which show – for example – the bombings to be militarily futile turn out – as Mr McNamara has demonstrated – to be politically irrelevant.

sentimentalists who complain about specific forms of casualty – such as the loss by children of eyes and reason – which are statistically predictable, and assimilable to known patterns of policy, then certain consequences follow. The characters of some of these advisers and their images of themselves become such that they will tend to advocate terrorism, *whether in reality it is likely to be profitable or not*, in order to demonstrate their own cold intellectuality. This is the type of adviser who can most easily find a living at present. And of course this kind of mind, perpetually confirming its own lack of squeamishness, will have an ever higher propensity to accumulate around the heads of the armed services than around the Presidency, thus giving rise to competition in cerebration about terrorism: a cerebration which is, however, in reality subordinate to the results of calculations about domestic politics.

Into the horrible calculus of these sick men, there necessarily enters however one limiting factor on which relatively normal human beings have some slight purchase. This is the growing disgust which the accumulated results of these calculations have caused in widening sections of the American public. While Johnson remains in the White House, this cannot be expected to do more than exercise a certain restraint – through the flickerings of that popularity rating – on the President and his entourage. If however – as seems to be happening – rejection of the war becomes more widespread, more determined and more open, then the next occupant of the White House is likely to be led to end the war in the only way, short of genocide, in which it can be ended: by the withdrawal of the American troops. (If this leads to a revival of McCarthyism, liberals will have a chance of showing their mettle.)

It is to be hoped that the documentary parts of Mr Gerassi's book, as well as his eye-witness accounts, will play a part in widening and intensifying the rejection of the war. His quotations from American sources – notably the Air Force's definition of 'psycho-social targets' – schools, hospitals, etc. – are even more horrifying in their implications than is the direct impact of what he reports. His book also contains a number of documents from North Vietnamese sources. The style of these documents, and a number of the historical and other assumptions on which they are based, are not likely to be acceptable to Americans. The public has been so conditioned as to combine a marked dread of contamination by Communist propaganda, with an equally marked willingness – now somewhat eroded – to accept Washington-manufactured propaganda as constituting news. The North Vietnam documents cited by Mr Gerassi are of course propaganda, as are the statements of Messrs McNamara, Rusk and others. American readers have had unlimited exposure to the propaganda of their own side. They should also study these presentations of the views of the North Vietnamese and the Front of National Liberation. Those should be considered in the light of the long war, bearing in mind that in this war so far the Americans – like the French before them – have been fighting only Vietnamese. Dean Rusk likes to talk about Chinese aggression, but the hundreds of thousands of foreign troops now laying waste Vietnam are neither Chinese nor Russian. They are the troops of the United States and her allies. The task they are attempting is the subjugation of the national resistance of a peasant country, through the fullest possible application of the intellectual, scientific, industrial and military resources of the wealthiest country in the world. The idea that perseverance in this enterprise of terrorism is conducive to the prestige of the United States is no longer plausible even in Washington. But in the meantime the population of Vietnam must continue to pay the price here described for the high ambitions they have thwarted and the high reputations they have injured.

Northern Ireland Observed

Decent people in England who have given earnest, but not very prolonged, thought to the Northern Ireland question sometimes come up with the thought that the solution would be the appointment of a Catholic Tory Lord as Executive Governor. The Catholics would love him for his religion, the Protestants for his politics. The process would be helped on by a combined visit of the Pope and the Archbishop of Canterbury, to recommend religious peace.

Direct contact with the area, and conversation with members of the two communities, brings the depressing discovery that a Catholic Tory would be the most unpopular of all possible governors. The Catholics, it is true, would not necessarily dislike him much more for being Catholic as well as Governor. If he were an English Catholic, the weight of additional dislike would hardly be perceptible, since the Catholicism of the English is not felt to be the same as the religion of the same name practised in Ireland. There would just be the embarrassment which is generally felt when a gesture intended to be agreeable falls flat. But if the new Governor were an *Irish* Catholic he would be regarded by many Catholics as a traitor – an Irishman representing an English monarch in Ireland – and would be high on the assassination lists. As for the Ulster Protestants, the appointment of a Catholic – of whatever provenance – as Executive Governor would appear to many of them as the worst insult and threat to the province since

The Times Literary Supplement, 17 March 1972. The books under review are: Richard Rose, *Governing Without Consensus: An Irish Perspective* (Faber, London, 1971); R. S. P. Elliot and John Hickie, *Ulster: A Case Study in Conflict Theory* (Longman, London, 1971); Constantine FitzGibbon, *Red Hand: The Ulster Colony* (Michael Joseph, London, 1971).

the reign of James II, and since the arch-traitor Lundy was governor of Londonderry.

So far as the Pope and the Archbishop of Canterbury are concerned, the undoubted pleasure of Belfast Catholics at seeing their Holy Father would be marred by the spectacle of tens of thousands of their fellow citizens trying to get at that venerated figure in order to drown him in the Lagan (together with the Archbishop for coming with the Pope, and thereby becoming, in Protestant eyes, what an Irish Catholic Governor would be in Irish Catholic eyes – a traitor). The whole ecumenical exercise, if carried out, would produce riots and mayhem on a scale far exceeding anything that even Belfast has yet known. Fortunately the Pope, whether infallible or not, has sense enough to keep out of Belfast.

Components and variants of the Catholic/Governor/Pope/ Archbishop cure have been heard from more than one Member of Parliament, and from a newspaper magnate. Their disaster-fraught suggestions were the result, not of stupidity or ill-will, but of superficial information. It is probable that if they had read the first of the three books reviewed here they would not have offered these suggestions, and indeed that they would have refrained altogether from utterance on this grim, complex and impracticable subject.

Richard Rose's *Governing Without Consensus* is probably the most illuminating book ever written about Northern Ireland. Its core is made up of the responses to what Professor Rose called a 'loyalty' survey carried out by him over 'a multi-stage stratified random sample of 1500 households'. The stratification of areas was 'by religion, partisanship, and urban, semi-urban or rural character'. A total of 757 Protestants and 534 Roman Catholics were interviewed: 58·6 per cent Protestants and 41·4 per cent Catholics – approximating to the actual balance of the two communities, with a slight inflation of the Catholic component.

The inflation is not significant for the survey, since results are presented separately for Protestant and Catholic respondents. It was carried out during the period March to August 1968. The results therefore relate to the last months of what we may now call 'the old Northern Ireland'. The period of the survey was not only before the coming of serious violence, but also before the

Civil Rights movement entered its active phase of non-violent militancy, in October 1968. It must not, therefore, be assumed that the attitudes recorded by Professor Rose are those now held by the same proportion of the two communities. In many cases they almost certainly are not: a hardening of attitudes in both communities, throughout the period between 1968 and 1972, is something which almost all observers agree in discerning. The true extent, character and distribution of what is vaguely described as 'hardening' could, however, only be found out by means of a new survey, conducted as closely as possible on the lines of Professor Rose's 1968 survey.

Fortunately Professor Rose was very happy in his choice of dates; a survey finished in the summer of 1968 forms the perfect baseline against which to measure the effects of the years of challenge and of violence. *Un*fortunately, it would probably not be safe to attempt such a survey either in present conditions, or in any conditions likely soon to exist in the province; and if a new survey were attempted its results might not be reliable. A climate of fear, suspicion, intimidation and violence is unfavourable to the carrying through of any kind of public opinion survey, but especially of one on so 'hot' a subject as loyalty.

The material in this long book – more than 550 pages including the notes – is rich in detail. No attempt will be made here to summarize a book which everyone seriously interested in Northern Ireland will want to read for themselves, but attention should be drawn to certain aspects of Professor Rose's findings which seem particularly significant.

The first concerns the degree of alienation of the Catholic minority from the Northern Ireland regime, in the forty-ninth year of that regime's existence. This survey shows that that alienation – while greater than certain Unionist spokesmen, in their more euphorically 'Rhodesian' moments, suggested – was less, indeed considerably less, than nationalist spokesmen were accustomed to claim. Professor Rose's single most startling finding is that 33 per cent said they approved the constitutional position of Northern Ireland; 34 per cent said they disapproved; 32 per cent said they didn't know. (We aren't told what happened to the other 1 per cent.) Among Protestants the proportions were: approve 68 per cent; disapprove 1 per cent; don't know

22 per cent (apparently Protestants are more amenable to being added up than Catholics are).

Even in 1968, 34 per cent was almost certainly inadequate as an index of Catholic alienation. Many of the 33 per cent 'don't knows' could probably be added to it. Professor Rose indicates they were 'persons of limited education', and it seems they just failed to understand a rather fancily worded question. But even if we make the extreme assumption that all the 'don't knows' can be lumped with the 'disapproves', we are still left with the fact, as it was then, of approval of the Northern Ireland Constitution by one-third of the Catholics. In present circumstances it may safely be assumed that the figure would be greatly reduced (1972: see note at end of essay.)

It might be thought that the 33 per cent who approved were the upper crust of the Catholic community. Other parts of the survey, however, show little reason to believe that there is much class difference between them and the 34 per cent 'disapproves' (although most of the 'don't knows' presumably fall in a lower class than either of the deciding groups). Professor Rose finds a strong correlation between political views and religion; and a weak correlation between political views and social class. These facts are of course obvious to anyone who has spent any time in Northern Ireland, but like many other obvious facts they have been partly concealed from view by a froth of rhetoric. Professor Rose blows away much of the froth.

In so far as class differences are more important than religious differences, Ulster people of the same class should have more similar regime outlooks than people of different classes but the same religion. The data from the loyalty surveys clearly reject this hypothesis. The difference between middle-class and working-class Protestants in support for the Constitution is 4 per cent and 3 per cent in endorsement of an ultra position. Similarly, among Catholics, there is only a 2 per cent difference across classes in support for the Constitution, and a 5 per cent difference in readiness to demonstrate against the regime. The differences between religions are much larger. Within the middle class, Protestants and Catholics differ by 36 percentage points in their readiness to support the Constitution. And manual workers differ by 30 percentage points. In refusal to comply with basic political laws, about half of each class group is ready to endorse extra-constitutional actions against others who share class but not regime outlooks. It is particularly noteworthy that there is no consistent tendency from middle-class Ulster people to be readiest to endorse the Constitution and refrain from extra-constitutional politics, notwithstanding their relative advantage in terms of status.

Governing Without Consensus is a rather depressing book – as any objective book on Northern Ireland has to be. One can pick from it, for consolation, two straws of potential hope. One is the fact that, whereas the Catholic hierarchy have rejected integrated education – Catholics and Protestants together – no less than 69 per cent of the Catholic part of Professor Rose's sample are in favour of integrated education. (This is, even so, a frail little straw, for the author also finds that 'while attendance at mixed schools tends to reduce ultra and rebel views, it does so only to a very limited extent'. The figures he cites, however, are a little more encouraging than his 'very limited' would suggest.)

The second relatively hopeful finding – and a much-needed ray of hope at the present time – is that people who recalled 'actively bad' community relations showed the least propensity to endorse violence. 'This suggests', says Professor Rose, 'that while sectarian bitterness will make people fighting mad, some who see its consequences in bloodshed and disorder will react against it.' Let us hope the 'some' will become 'many'.

The factual content of *Governing Without Consensus* is presented with admirable lucidity and fairness. Professor Rose's theoretical formulations based on the material seem to be less satisfactory, being both over-elaborate and excessively noncommittal; a combination favoured by too many social scientists. There is one other small carp. The photographs included relate mainly to a period later than the loyalty survey, and may mislead the unwary reader by their topicality. Professor Rose does comment on events later then 1968, but it is from the survey he then directed that all the attitudes analysed by him are taken. Yet the merits of this book overwhelmingly outweigh its deficiencies, and all concerned with Northern Ireland owe a deep debt of gratitude to Professor Rose.

Ulster: A Case Study of Conflict Theory is the kind of book that brings conflict theory studies into disrepute. The authors set out by raising hopes that they are about to bring to bear on the Northern Ireland conflict more precise and sensitive terminology and more rigorous methods than have yet been applied to it. We could do with this. But in reality nothing is brought to bear on anything. The book consists in the main of slices of theoretical verbiage alternating with slices of popular and highly inaccurate history and social description. There is little or no interpenetration between the theoretical bit and the narrative-and-descriptive bits, and the conclusions, so far as they concern Ulster, are not based either on the theory or on the narrative. Some of them are merely the sort of thing the weariest leader-writer could have thought up without 'scientific' assistance: 'This indicates that until constructive steps are taken it seems unlikely that there will be any progress in relations between the two communities and therefore in bringing an end to the trouble.' Others are mere wish-fulfilments, flying in the face of the observed facts: 'This is because there is now a chance of radical re-structuring of the political division – away from religion, toward a class framework.'

The book also contains the insignificant results of an embarrassingly amateurish survey conducted in March 1969, by means of interviews with some politicians in Belfast and a few in Dublin. The politicians talked their heads off, it seems, and the interviewers, having neither shorthand nor tape-recorders, wrote down bits here and there. 'All the answers', the authors disarmingly observe, 'are an edited version distorted in terms of what the interviewer thought most important.'

The interviewers could scarcely have been competent to edit this material nor would the authors have been competent, because they do not seem to know their chosen field of study well enough, as appears at many points. That they mugged up their subject hastily and approximately is shown, for example, by a reference to 'the 1789 Irish Socialist uprising'; the statement that 'during the war Southern Ireland gave support to the German cause and it was then [sic] that the slogan "England's danger is Eire's [sic] opportunity" was coined'; by the appearance of distorted proper names like 'Warroughk' and 'Whittacker'; by the definition of the Dáil as 'the Dublin Houses of Parliament', as well as by more subtle evidences of unfamiliarity. Moreover, the standard of

H.—D

proof-reading is so bad that it is often hard to know whether the authors mean what they actually appear to be saying, or the opposite, or something in between: for instance, 'cases of violent conflict between communities of roughly the same size are rarer than those where there is equality'. On the whole, 'inequality' seems the more likely reading.

Red Hand': The Ulster Colony is a rather easy-going informal discussion of the historical roots of Northern Ireland. Many people are likely to find it readable and informative, while regretting Constantine FitzGibbon's tendency to skip from period to period, with very little notice: and his frequent and rather strange comparisons with outside phenomena. Very little of this book deals with contemporary Northern Ireland, and Mr Fitz-Gibbon is not at his best in this section: 'It would seem that the Red IRA being now under the control of International Communism as directed from Moscow, has been ordered to hold its hand for the time being. . . .' In fact it does not appear that either the 'Green' or the 'Red' IRA is under the control of anything – certainly not of anything so remote and exotic as 'International Communism . . . directed from Moscow'. This is the equivalent of the theory that the men of 1916 were in the pay of Berlin. In reality, Irish rebels have responded to Irish situations in their own way, sometimes borrowing rhetoric or ideology from abroad, and often looking there for weapons and other aid, but seldom amenable to outside advice. In any case, Moscow, like Rome (or even Dublin), would find it difficult to assess each crisis arising in Ardoyne or Andersonstown in time for its advice to have much relevance. Things move quickly, under pressure of local competition.

Author's note (1978): The above was written before the pro-rogation/abolition of Stormont. It cannot, I think, now 'safely be assumed' that the proportion of Catholics willing to accept the *present* status quo – direct rule from Britain – is lower than Professor Rose's 33 per cent.

The Catholic Church and the IRA

Recently an English political visitor asked me: 'Why doesn't the Church excommunicate the IRA?'

I told him the Church *had* excommunicated the IRA, in 1922. One of the persons then excommunicated is now the President of Ireland.*

Church leaders, throughout the nineteenth century, set their faces against the physical force movement. In the latter part of the century they used their spiritual authority against the Irish Republican Brotherhood (Fenians), making membership in a secret oath-bound society a reserved sin, from which only the Ordinary of the Diocese could absolve.

The effect of these measures, at the time of their application, is uncertain, and now an academic matter which may be left to the historians.

What is certain, and of practical contemporary significance, is the bearing which these past transactions have on the balance of forces between the Church and the IRA in our own day. This effect is enormously to undermine the authority of the Church in its dealings with the IRA and with patriotic violence generally.

The reason for this is that the Fenians *won*, or if they did not exactly win, came to be deemed the winners, which amounts in practice to much the same thing.

It was the Military Council of the Irish Republican Brotherhood, that organization so often condemned by the Church, which ordered the Rising of 1916. That Rising was itself condemned by Church leaders. However, after the execution of the 1916 leaders,

*Eamon de Valera.

and after the conscription crisis of 1917, the Irish people, in 1918, gave an overwhelming electoral majority to Sinn Fein, a party strongly influenced by the IRB, and dedicated to a cult of the Rising of 1916, as an act not only of high courage – which nobody could deny – but also one of transcendent political wisdom and virtue.

This very severe blow to the authority of the Church was masked in various ways. The body which had won, officially, was not the IRA but the more amorphous Sinn Fein, which was not secret, not oath-bound, and not condemned, and which had in fact been supported by certain Church leaders.

Nothing, however, could alter the fact that Sinn Fein derived all its prestige from the participation of its most prominent members in a rising ordered by the condemned IRB. The people seemed to have retrospectively approved the wisdom of the IRB, in the political area, as against the authority of the Church. The victory of Sinn Fein ensured that the independent Irish State soon to emerge – and to be dominated right up to 1973, and presumably beyond, by one or other wing of the old Sinn Fein – was to be committed to a cult of 1916. That is to say that the handiwork of an organization condemned by the Church was to become sacrosanct – and it is not too strong a word – in a country of practising and believing Catholics.

Some priests chafed at this situation, usually in silence.* Most acquiesced in it. By some a distinction was drawn: 'Sinn Fein, yes. IRB, no.' This drew a veil of the equivocal over the relation between the Church and the Republican movement, and that veil too remains part of the scene today.

The authority of the Church was further weakened, though this was not apparent at the time, by the events of 1922, when those who 'carried on the fight' against the Anglo-Irish treaty of 1921 were condemned and excommunicated. Here the Church was backing one wing of the 1916-based Sinn Fein against the other. But if the Rising of 1916, against utterly hopeless odds and

---

*In the summer of 1972 the Jesuit periodical *Studies* published an article entitled 'The Canon of Irish History – A Challenge' by Father Francis Shaw s.j. which was a strong attack on the cult of 1916 and Pearse in particular. The article had been written some years earlier in the commemorative year 1966 but had been suppressed at that time.

against the will of the elected representatives of the Irish people, had been right, it was hard to see on what moral grounds the Rising of 1922, militarily a little less hopeless, and supported by a strong minority of the elected representatives, should be condemned. The Republicans, though defeated, appeared to many as brave and patriotic men, fully in the line of 1916, unjustly persecuted by Churchmen who had appeared to give at least retrospective endorsement to the 1916 Rising. If they had not meant to endorse, why had they not condemned Sinn Fein?

The authority of the Church in this area was still further weakened when the party of those defeated and excommunicated in 1922 was returned to power in 1932. That party, Fianna Fáil, has been in power ever since, with the exception of two three-year coalitions of its opponents. It has of course never repudiated, but on the contrary glories in, the course of action for which its founder and his comrades were excommunicated in 1922.

Thus, history and the myths which history generates have combined to make the area of patriotic violence a privileged area into which the authority of the Church does not effectively penetrate. The Proclamation of the Republic, of which framed copies are in schools and state offices, implicitly but clearly asserts the sovereign immunity of patriotism-in-arms from the control of the Church, as well as from democratic control. In many other areas of Irish life the Church is very powerful: on this area it is almost impotent.

Anyone who understands this background will be rather slow to criticize harshly the dealings of present-day Irish Churchmen with the problem of the contemporary IRA. The Church leaders of today are handicapped both by the long history of this question and by their own long, if somewhat sullen, acquiescence in a state historical cult which repudiates several generations of their predecessors, and places patriotic violence outside the area in which their authority is deemed effective.

We do not know why the two Archbishops visited the sickbed of Mr Sean Mac Stiofain.* This may have derived in some form from the old rule about secret and oath-bound societies. However

---

*Mac Stiofain, formerly 'Chief of Staff' of the IRA, was visited when on hunger strike by the former Archbishop of Dublin, John Charles McQuaid, and by the present Archbishop, Dermot Ryan.

that may be, it would seem that whatever ecclesiastical regulation may necessitate the attendance of high ecclesiasticals (as distinct from ordinary priests) on such IRA leaders should be dropped. The visits reinforced extreme Protestants in their erroneous but quite sincere belief that the IRA is the arm of the Catholic Church. For that reinforcement – expressed and exploited on the front page of Mr Paisley's *Protestant Telegraph* – ordinary Catholics may have to pay with their lives, which are quite as valuable as that of Mr Mac Stiofain.

As far as condemning violence is concerned, the Northern Bishops at least have done as much as could reasonably be expected of them, granted the background. The Southern Bishops (with perhaps two exceptions) have so far been significantly less vocal. They do not seem to have done much to discourage the kind of chapel-gate collections for 'aid to the North', whose aid is likely to emerge in the form of the bomb and the bullet – and produce retaliation in similar terms. One can of course pretend not to know that is what the 'aid' is for; in political matters some of our clergy have learned to be good agnostics.

At a deeper level, the Catholic Church in Ireland, through its past attitudes, shares the responsibility for the culture that produced the IRA and this in three main ways.

First, in encouraging over many years a mood of tribal-sectarian 'holier than thou' self-righteousness and aversion from contact with 'non-Catholics'. (The Protestant Churches, on their side, encouraged the equivalents of these attitudes, but I am not directly concerned with them here.) On this Catholic nationalism the Provos grew up.

Second, in an authoritarian attitude, discouraging criticism and questioning, in education. When it happened that, as shown above, the Church abandoned *de facto* control over one area of indoctrination, that of patriotic violence, then the political cult introduced into that area was received in the same passive and unquestioning way as that in which the Church had encouraged the flock to receive all teaching which it sanctioned. And that passive receptivity helped the IRA.

Third, in preferring authoritarian methods – 'condemn', 'excommunicate' – to open, rational, public discussion as a means of turning people away from violence. The use of the second method would have required a challenge to the official ideology of the state. That challenge should not have been shirked.

It would be as wrong to blame the clergy of today for the failures of the past as it would be to blame Mr Whitelaw for the sack of Drogheda. Undoubtedly there is a movement now in the Church towards a re-examination of these matters. There is an equivalent movement among the Protestant Churches. If this ominous year, 1973, can pass without major disaster, these movements may be able to interact and bring us what we all most need: which is not political unification but the capacity to share an island without frightening one another to death.

A Yankee at the Court of
Queen Bernadette

The point is that a New York cop, Dermot Davey, visits Northern Ireland, and finds that there the Irish Catholics are the
niggers. The cops are the British Army and the Royal Ulster
Constabulary. He identifies with these niggers, against these cops,
and goes back to New York a better man. We see him, in an
Epilogue, performing an act of kindness for a black man.

The equation of Catholics and niggers is repeatedly brought
home. Dermot sees it for himself: 'The soldier held the boy by
the hair. Dermot had seen it all his life. The gun in a nigger's
ear.'

He is also told about it by his left-wing Catholic girlfriend-to-
be in Northern Ireland:

She gave him another cigarette. 'Do you not go around doing this to
people in America?' she said.
'The hell I do.'
'Ah Jesus now, come on. The whole fookin' police force in America
gets medals for shootin' blacks.'
'What are you talking about?'
'Are not the blacks at the bottom in America?'
'I don't know what you mean by the bottom.'
'The fookin' blacks are on the fookin' bottom and the fookin'
police beat them bloody, the same as we're on the bottom here and
the fookin' police and the fookin' soldiers beat us and shoot us like
animals.'

Dermot resists this imputation, then remembers a brutality
he had himself inflicted on a black boy in Knickerbocker Avenue:

Review in *New York Review of Books* of Jimmy Breslin, *World Without End,
Amen: A Novel* (Viking, New York, 1973; Hutchinson, London, 1974).

'He sat on the floor and thought about it for a moment. No, Dermot told himself, that was different from this. That was a nigger kid who stole something.'

He goes on drinking with the Catholic left; a tribe whose males, it seems, are a pretty cowardly lot, but whose women are charming, spirited and intelligent. Back home in Queens, Dermot had been a bit of a slob, whose gun had to be taken off him at intervals, but here he does various brave acts on behalf of the oppressed Catholics (blacks) without even thinking about it. He even sees how to see cops as pigs: 'A cop, pink cheeks sticking out from under his black hat – Christ, Dermot said to himself, the cops in Northern Ireland do look like pigs – had come up behind the bench.'

Dermot's regeneration proceeds apace. He administers a sound thrashing to an unworthy swain – though left-wing, yet of British origin – and gets the girl:

Ronald slouched into the bar, his head hanging. Dermot stepped out of the way to let him go through. Then he came in after him. Dermot kept his head down and didn't look up. He looked at Ronald's rear and kept looking at it. He didn't bring the head up, and he kicked him. It was a hard kick, a real hard kick, and Ronald went across the empty lounge to the back of it. He was half paralyzed for a moment and Dermot came right up and gave him another, this one a hell of a kick. It drove Ronald right to the door leading to the alley. He stumbled out the door and Dermot was all over him, shoving him so he would go down toward the office. Deirdre would see him. Ronald started down the alley. Dermot kept his head down. Ronald ran and Dermot ran after him and kicked him again. He didn't look at him. He turned around at the finish of the kick and went out and waited by the car. Deirdre came around from the courthouse running. He held the car door for her.

Deirdre, with Dermot, campaigns for Bernadette Devlin.

The girl talking on the truck really was just a little girl. Long straight hair down the sides of an oval face and a teenage bad tooth. But her blue eyes were old. She was in a red dress that was as short as you could get it. She finished to loud cheering and clapping from the ones on her side of the street. The ones across the street were shaking their fists.

At the election meeting, Deirdre gets shot dead. Who shot her is not made clear, except that it was someone who was aiming at Bernadette: 'they was aiming at herself and they get the goddam poor wrong one.' The careless reader, who will enjoy the book most, will assume that the British Army did it: what is implied in fact is that Protestant extremists did it, but the distinction between the two elements has been lost in the general rhetoric of the book. Ironically, Bernadette herself leaves under Army guard.

The candidate, a cigarette in her mouth, eyes straight ahead, walked past the soldiers and slipped into a car. As the car started off, somebody pulled the guitar in through the window. A jeep rocked to a halt in the middle of the street. The driver shouted. The two soldiers, keeping Dermot in the alley, left him. The soldiers ran out to the jeep and swung onto the back. The jeep jumped forward and started after the car with the candidate in it.

It is perhaps necessary to remind the reader, that though the candidate is identifiable, and the election campaign real – the elections for the United Kingdom parliament in the summer of 1970 – the incident itself is fictitious, and so also is the behaviour of the candidate. Even those in Ireland who – like the reviewer – are not political admirers of Miss Devlin's will also think this behaviour out of character. In fact, the author of *World Without End, Amen* seems to have a love-hate relationship towards Miss Devlin. The heroine Deirdre is lovably bernadettesque, beautiful and a martyr to boot: 'the candidate', depicted with the physical characteristics and political circumstances of Bernadette herself, is a cold little turkey according to Dermot, and is given an appropriate exit.

According to the jacket of *World Without End, Amen* 'with his characteristic no-nonsense approach to reporting, Mr Breslin has created a fiction which is far more revealing than mere facts can ever be even at their most unadorned'.

I understand that in the United States *World Without End, Amen* is rather widely taken to be a revelation of the nature and origin of the troubles in Northern Ireland. There are reasons for being sceptical about this revelation. Certainly anyone who tries to understand the situation in Northern Ireland today with the aid of Mr Breslin's book will find himself or herself far out at sea. This novel is set in Northern Ireland in a particular very short period – the summer of 1970 – before the Provisional IRA started killing (there were twenty dead through political violence by the end of 1970: today there are nearly one thousand).

The revelation of *World Without End, Amen* consists of naturalistic, though not altogether unadorned, descriptions of riots and other incidents, interspersed with dialogue and speeches almost all of which reflect the interpretation of the situation offered by the left-wing 'Official' IRA and its propagandists, including Miss Devlin. The reason why this account strikes so many unfamiliar with the scene as revealing is that both the riot descriptions and the rhetoric are in fact familiar: the language of the 'Official' IRA is the language of the international left. The elements in the Northern Ireland political situation which are peculiar to it, and therefore essential to an understanding of it, are either left out (both in 'Official' rhetoric and in the book) or shrunken into meaninglessness. The peculiarities of Northern Ireland surface, in the book, only in the apolitical and acceptable form of local colour, which Mr Breslin lays on with gusto and some skill. Under this formula the reader can feel he understands everything without really having to think about it.

In fact no element in Northern Ireland is treated at all adequately in *World Without End, Amen* except the left-wing Catholics: that is to say a tiny minority out of a sizeable minority – and these are treated adequately only in the sense that their rhetoric is lavishly reproduced. The Protestants, who are the majority of the population of Northern Ireland, are seen as through the wrong end of a telescope: small, nasty figures, easily identifiable with 'Southern Whites'. The sort of Catholics who form the whole of the elected representation of the Catholics of Northern Ireland – and who are denounced by both wings of the IRA – do not appear at all. The Provisionals, the larger and more deadly end of the IRA, make only the sketchiest and most uncertain of appearances, and are the object of ambiguous utterances by the 'Official' heroine. The British Army's role is grossly over-simplified. No reader of this book would be likely to realize that that Army had been deployed to protect the Catholics – and was warmly welcomed by them – in August

1969 and that if it had been withdrawn in the period Mr Breslin describes, large numbers of Catholics in Belfast would have been massacred, as they would also now.

The picture of that Army's role as one of simple support for the class status quo is, again, 'Official' IRA rhetoric. The Protestant loyalist rhetoric, according to which the Army was misused to overthrow Protestant ascendancy in Ulster, is considerably nearer the mark. Analogies illuminate only to mislead, but if any American analogy to the role of the British Army in Ulster in 1969–70 is to be found, the use of Federal troops at Little Rock, Arkansas, by President Eisenhower in 1957 is much closer than Mr Breslin's white cops in Harlem. But for subsequent developments – notably the deliberate and successful efforts by both wings of the IRA to provoke hostilities between the British Army and the Catholic population generally – there is no American analogy. (Incidentally Mr Breslin at one point in his book describes such IRA efforts which he must have witnessed in Derry and the use of children in them: in the rhetorical context, however, few readers are likely to understand exactly what is being described.)

As a political guide to the Northern Ireland situation, either in 1970, 1974 or at any other time, *World Without End, Amen* is worse than useless, since it is plausibly and persistently misleading. Considering it as a work of fiction, I do not find it any more satisfactory. I cannot believe in Dermot Davey, either as the brutal moronic racist stock cop in Queens in the first part of the book, or as the brave and resourceful Yankee at the Court of Queen Bernie in the second. Nor can I see any connection between the two characters. The idea that suddenly seeing Catholics as niggers produces spiritual regeneration in racist Irish cops strikes me as not the least among the book's flutters in silly fantasy. I have met not a few Irish-Americans, with the ordinary Athletic Club racist outlooks, who had been to Northern Ireland, and who sincerely sympathized with the oppressed Catholics there. And they saw the analogy all right. They saw Irishmen being treated as niggers and they objected to them being treated as niggers, because they were *not* niggers. *That* was what was wrong. I do not believe that the Dermot Davey depicted in the first part of this book could have seen the situation in any other light. Nor do I believe he would have spent all that time among all those left-wing intellectuals (unless of course he was working for the CIA).

Left to himself, Dermot, if he had got there at all, which is not likely, would have gravitated to the Provos: straightforward no-nonsense patriotic Catholic killers. It is Jimmy Breslin, not any possible Dermot Davey, who finds the 'Officials' and semi-'Officials' interesting and convincing. And Dermot, as the vehicle for Jimmy Breslin's impressions in Northern Ireland, turns into something very like Jimmy's impression of Breslin.

The pity of it is that Mr Breslin could have written quite a good book about Northern Ireland; vestiges of it are embedded in *World Without End, Amen*. He is a reporter who describes very well what he actually sees: his descriptions of riots, of the outward appearance of people and their clothes, of houses, rooms, bars and streets, are accurate and telling. (His *ear* is much less good: most of his Irish dialogue is unspeakable, in every sense of the word.) If he had put his meagre ideological equipment on the shelf, had put cottonwool in his ears, and had described what he actually saw in Northern Ireland that summer, day by day, the result would have had to be much nearer to the truth, and also more interesting, than *World Without End, Amen*.

Broadcasting and Terrorism

Any legislation on broadcasting, even limited amending legislation, as at present, necessarily raises very fundamental issues: essentially those of freedom in a democratic state and the limits of such freedom.

When the original Bill was debated, there was relatively little discussion of these fundamental issues and the debate concentrated on the more immediate and practical aspects of the legislation, which was of course generally, and in the main rightly, welcomed.

There was, I believe, still at that time in our legislature a certain reluctance to discuss fundamental issues, based – as often among us – on the contradictory but simultaneously held assumptions that we all, as decent people, thought alike on these matters, *and* that it would be dangerously divisive to discuss them. These assumptions and the habits generated by them still linger in various departments of our national life, but the degree to which they inhibit parliamentary debate is very much reduced. The way is open for us now, if we wish, to debate these matters in a more ample and far-ranging way than would have seemed appropriate in the past.

I think it is right that we should do so, and I hope that Senators may agree with me on this point at least.

I would hope that, when we come to discuss the Bill in detail, and amendments to it, that debate will have been illuminated in advance by a thorough discussion of the basic principles involved. That discussion may appropriately take place at this stage of the consideration of the Bill, and it is that discussion I now wish to

From a speech by the author, as Minister for Posts and Telegraphs, in the Irish Senate introducing the Broadcasting Authority (Amendment) Bill, 27 March 1975.

initiate. I hope that as I approach these very large questions, unavoidably touching on central issues of political philosophy, Senators will not feel that I am in any way attempting to lay down the law to them. It is for the Oireachtas★ to lay down the law, and quite literally so. As Minister I am simply bringing before the Senate, as a contribution to the discussion, my own view of the principles involved in such legislation. Some Senators may well support and seek to improve the Bill, as a reasonably workman-like measure, while not choosing to follow into the more speculative area which I am now entering, or indeed while rejecting some of my formulations of the principles involved.

Others may on the whole accept these formulations but feel that the Bill itself does not adequately correspond to them. Both points of view and others could enrich the debate and help to chasten and improve the Bill.

The seven basic questions which I would put, and to which I would offer tentative answers for your examination, are the following:

Has the democratic state the right to pass repressive legislation? Has it the right to restrict freedom of expression? If so, what limitations should apply to such rights? Should the state have greater rights of restriction in relation to broadcasting than to the press? What limitations should there be on the state's right to intervene in broadcasting? When we speak of freedom in broadcasting, whose freedom do we mean and how is it to be defended? Finally, whatever principles we hold valid in relation to these general questions, are there any special circumstances prevailing in our society in our time which make it necessary or prudent to apply these principles in particular ways?

As regards the first question, I don't suppose there can be many members of this or any other legislature who hold the doctrine that the state should *never* engage in any kind of repressive legislation. Most of our laws seek to repress something or other, whether it be abuse of drugs, exposure of workers to unnecessary

★Parliament.

risks, ill-treatment of children, murder or other undesirable practices.

The reason I raise this question first is that, in the form of a pejorative slogan, it has very often been launched against the legislation I am seeking to amend, and will certainly be launched against some parts of the amending legislation. There are of course weighty arguments against such legislation as I am now introducing, and I shall come to these. But I begin with this particular argument, which is clearly invalid, because I am concerned about the implications of its fairly wide use, especially among young people. Those who use this slogan suggest that, whenever the liberal and democratic state uses repressive legislation, backed as it has to be by the power to coerce those who will not obey the laws, that then it is departing from its own principles. The underlying argument which has often been used by fascists and Communists, but is also used by others, is that the liberal and democratic state, by reason of its own principles, has no right to defend itself, or the citizens who look to it for their defence. This is of course an invitation to the liberal and democratic state to commit suicide. It may be asked in parenthesis whether ours actually *is* a liberal and democratic state. It is, I would say, as democratic as the most democratic country in the world, and about as liberal as that democracy is prepared to stand. It is less liberal than other Western European countries but is undoubtedly growing more liberal than it was. Unfortunately the wish to be liberal, or to demand liberalism from others, is often accompanied by only the vaguest notions of what liberalism is, as the slogans about repressive legislation show. The debate now opening would be particularly useful if it helped to clarify ideas in that regard. The simple principle which came to be at the heart of the liberal democratic state was laid down for Athens more than two thousand years ago:

> Neither excess of rule nor anarchy
> That is the mean my townsmen shall observe.

All liberal and democratic states have tried to observe that mean, always differing strongly within themselves as to what particular measures may involve 'excess of rule' and what may lead to 'anarchy', but always accepting that anarchy is to be abhorred and that the state must maintain, and where necessary use, an apparatus of repression. It may be well to distinguish here between what one might call practical work-a-day anarchy and the anarchy of the philosophical anarchists. The latter would be a highly desirable thing, if the assumptions on which it were based were true, or could become true. And of course they may one day come true. It may come about, as a result of technological developments, and wiser use of that technology, stabilization of world population, elimination of poverty, vastly improved education and understanding of our own psychology, that aggression, cruelty, greed and exploitation of the weak by the strong will disappear altogether from human behaviour and all people will devote their energies to helping one another, rather than winning advantages for themselves. In those conditions, anarchy would be a benign state of affairs and repressive legislation would be unthinkable. Whether humanity as a whole may conceivably be moved in that direction I would not care to guess: the question is related to that of the perfectability of man, and might bring us to the perilous fringes of theology. But we are certainly nowhere near such a Utopian state of affairs now, and this country is not noticeably nearer to it than any other country. In present conditions, human nature and the human situation being as they are, anarchy – that is, the breakdown of the state – simply involves disseminated retail-tyranny: forms of rule unchecked either by civilized tradition or by constitutional or conventional safeguards of any kind.

I have encountered, in different parts of Africa at different times, in parts of a great American city, and more recently in parts of Northern Ireland, situations in which the gunman for a time is absolute ruler over a given area, fairly large or very small: where the gunman's mind is the sole legislature and judicature, and his armed hand the executive. In comparison to conditions in these squalid and barbarous little empires, the abuses which prevail in the daylight of the effective jurisdiction of a democratic state, serious as they are in absolute terms, pale into relative insignificance. The democratic state has the duty to defend itself and those whom it represents against such threats and such encroachments, and the duty moreover to do so effectively. It has the duty also to defend and where possible extend the general liberties of the citizens to the maximum extent compatible with the secure survival of that on which both the liberties themselves and the prospect of their growth ultimately depend: that is, the democratic state itself. There is obviously a tightrope situation here: the democratic state has to save itself on the one hand from being pushed by fear of anarchy into 'excess of rule' and on the other hand to save itself from falling into anarchy through fear of excess of rule. This is a perennial problem. How the balance is best kept at any time and in any place depends on one's judgement of the circumstances prevailing. I shall come later to the question that concerns us most closely: the application of these principles to our own situation, and the balance most appropriate to our conditions.

I imagine that all Senators, or almost all, will agree in general with the answers to that first question: that the democratic state has the right to enact repressive legislation, provided that it represses the right things in the right way, and by means that are adequate but not excessive. Opinions may well be more divided on the second question: Has the state the right to restrict freedom of expression? It is possible to hold that it is best not to do so at all: that the state should restrain, where necessary, overt and material actions, but should leave purely verbal utterances strictly alone. Language, it is argued, can be a safety valve for feelings which might otherwise find more dangerous expression; debate, using even the most heated forms of argument, has a cleansing power; even the most detestable ideas – the advocacy of genocide, for example – should be allowed the widest possible expression, and then be met by reasoned argument. This is undoubtedly an attractive concept, especially to those who have an absolute faith in the force of rational argument, as capable of overcoming appeals to the passions. Those who hold to this view often quote with approval certain well-known lines of John Milton, including the famous 'Let her [truth] and falsehood grapple! Who ever knew truth put to the worse in a free and open encounter?'

This and other fine sayings have been adduced, to support a doctrine that freedom of expression is an absolute, whose untrammelled exercise will necessarily be beneficial to society and that the state has no right to interfere with it. The weakness of the doctrine is that it tends to assume that all discourse consists of rational argument and to ignore the rather obvious fact, not unfamiliar to us in this country, that a word can lead to a blow.

In wider terms, language can be used to inflict pain and arouse cruelty; to instil fear into one group and arouse hatred in another; it can be used to whip up feelings conducive to pogroms; it can be used to exploit revulsion against one atrocity in order to justify the commission of other atrocities; it can be used to legitimize a sustained campaign of violence, to raise funds for that campaign and to confuse or intimidate those who tend to question or oppose such a campaign.

Incidentally Milton, who did not in fact favour absolute freedom to publish with impunity, was well aware of the violence with which words can be charged. 'Books', he wrote, 'are as lively and as vigorously productive as those fabulous Dragon's teeth: and being sown up and down may chance to spring up armed men.' What was true of the printed word in the seventeenth century is certainly no less true of the words far more widely 'sown up and down' today by broadcasting. An emotional appeal is not capable of being dispelled by rational argument alone. An insult, backed by a threat, is not adequately answered by a syllogism. For these and related reasons all states, even the most liberal, have in fact placed some restraints on freedom of expression and indeed liberal states continue to add new restrictions, notably, and rightly, in the field of racially offensive language. The effectiveness of such restrictions is open to question – as is the effectiveness of laws in general – but the placing of legal curbs on defamation, insults, threats, incitement to violence and racial smears is generally accepted as having on the whole salutary effects, as tending to establish desirable norms of behaviour and as being conducive to the peace of society and the well-being of individuals and families. Words are in fact an integral part of many patterns of action. If this is accepted, the absolute distinction between words and actions is broken down, and words and actions together become part of a pattern of behaviour which is and should be amenable to law.

If we accept, then, that *some* restrictions may be applied to freedom of expression, we come to our third question: What limitations should apply to such restrictions? A line which one might legitimately seek to draw – though it is very hard in

practice – is that which would set apart, as belonging to the
sphere of action amenable to law, all forms of play on the emotions, through words and images, in ways likely to arouse fear
and hatred, to cause acute distress, or to endanger the lives of
citizens, and the security of the state responsible for those lives.
All other forms of discourse should be the domain of freedom of
expression. Any restriction on freedom of speech should have to
be shown to be desirable in the general interests, not just the
interest of the Government of the day. Not merely its formal
wording, but its actual working should be exposed to continued
scrutiny and to renewed debate, so as to ensure that a restriction
accepted for the protection of the citizens is not abused for the
exclusive benefit of their rulers. I hope this new legislation meets
these tests. I am certain that it meets them better than the legislative provisions which it replaces.

Coming now more closely to the nub of our discussion here, we
consider the fourth question, that of what particular rights the
state should legitimately exercise in relation to broadcasting, and
in particular what restrictions the state may legitimately require
in this sphere. Our democratic state does, for example, exert
much greater control over broadcasting than over the press. This
arises from the nature of the situation: the fact that the electro-
magnetic spectrum, unlike newsprint and ink, is public property
and cannot readily be bought and sold in separate consignments
and that therefore broadcasting has to be controlled, in some
degree at least, by the state on behalf of the community, basically
through an inherent monopoly in the allocation of frequencies,
combined with responsibility to the people in the matter of how
these frequencies are used.

If the state allocates the use of a public asset and if it requires
citizens who wish to benefit from use of that asset, to pay for
their privilege, then the state, on behalf of the citizens who both
pay the licence fees and elect the Government of the state, has a
particular responsibility in relation to broadcasting, and specifically the responsibility to ensure that broadcasting is not used to
endanger either the security of the state which licensed it, or the
lives of the citizens who pay for it. These considerations are greatly
reinforced by the fact that broadcasting, of all the media, both
through sounds and images, has by far the most immediate

impact on people and situations, has by far the greatest capacity to generate emotion, and that its capacities in these regards have aroused and held the fascinated attention of people interested in promoting and justifying violence, and strongly desirous of access to broadcasting for these ends. Professional broadcasters have themselves publicly noted that in certain conditions the mere appearance of a television camera on a street may tend to speed up the action of a riot – the speeding up being clearly aimed at the television camera and through it at television screens throughout the area, the presumed object and probable effect of this being to spread similar patterns of conduct more widely. . . .

This brings us to the fifth question of what limitations there should be on the state's right to intervene. As in other cases the power to regulate needs itself to be regulated carefully so that the response is not excessive and that broadcasting remains free to cover the flow of news adequately and to discuss current affairs intelligently, probingly, comprehensively and with access to a very wide range of opinion. The difficulties involved here are probably never entirely soluble. Dr Johnson implied as much when he wrote: 'The danger of such unbounded liberty, and the danger of bounding it have produced a problem in the science of government, which human understanding seems hitherto unable to solve.' I hope the Senate will take that durable 'hitherto' as a challenge.

This question of the limitation on the state's right to intervene is closely linked to my sixth question: When we speak of freedom in broadcasting, whose freedom do we mean and how is it to be defended? Some people – quite a few people indeed – have written and spoken as if implying that freedom of broadcasting meant the freedom of any individual broadcaster to broadcast just what he liked. It is not easy to see how this could be defended; to begin with, the general considerations I have already mentioned apply here too. If an individual broadcaster takes it into his head to engage in hate-propaganda against a minority, or a majority for that matter, there ought to be someone there to stop him – at least if we accept the essentials of the foregoing argument. In broadcasting, as in other forms of collective activity – in newspapers, for example – no individual is entirely free to do what he

likes: and as in every valid, creative, collective enterprise, each
individual involved in the creative process has a considerable
say in what goes on: that is, the freedom involved is a collective
freedom, under law.

There is no doubt that this kind of freedom would be – and
was here for some considerable time – stifled by direct day-to-day
governmental control over broadcasting – the system which the
late Erskine Childers ended. It could also be damaged by indirect
covert governmental pressure, exercised nominally in the public
interest, but actually in the interests of a person or persons
holding power at a given moment in time. Broadcasters have to
be protected from that type of interference, just as the public has
to be protected against the possible use of broadcasting in support
of violent groups hostile to democracy by the exploitation of
emotions, through the use of words and images, in such a way
as to promote the objectives of such groups. I believe that on the
whole the present structures, whereby the Director General is
nominated by and responsible to an Authority nominated by the
elected Government, have tended in general to serve these two
purposes – never wholly compatible or wholly attainable – of
protecting both the public and the broadcasters. But I believe
also that these structures can be improved by defining what
might be called the reserve powers retained by the Government
and Parliament as relating to security – and security only – and
by doing everything possible to eliminate the danger of covert
interference for reasons other than those basic reasons on which
I have laid stress here.

I believe that the strengthening of the Authority, and the
clarifying of its relation to the state, are in fact the best means
both of upholding the collective freedom of broadcasting and
the principle of responsibility to the state. That, at any rate, is the
objective sought in this part of the legislation soon to be open for
discussion here.

The final question which I posed and which I would now like
to discuss, is that of whether any special circumstances prevail in
our society in our time which make it necessary or prudent to
apply these principles in particular ways?

I think our history, both in the more remote past and recently,
has placed us today in a situation where the defence of the

democratic state, together with the liberal values and civil rights for all citizens which that kind of state alone sustains, requires a high degree of intelligent vigilance and that such vigilance should be turned on our use of words and images and particularly on the broadcasting of these.

Our Irish relation to democracy involves elements which we hold in common with the citizens of other democracies, and also other elements peculiar to our own condition, which in turn give a special tincture even to that which seems to be held in common. Like many other citizens of democracies, we practise democracy, but we do not greatly esteem it. We are extremely conscious of its failings, which are many. We see its ridiculous side – and we in Ireland perhaps see that more persistently than most – and certainly that side is there. We elect our representatives, but then we treat them like scapegoats, and rather shabby scapegoats at that. The casual, rather slighting relation of the citizen to the state is a part of democratic life, and even a part of why we value democracy. This is the only form of government in which the citizens can with impunity treat their rulers with contempt, and this is no small part of its drab but real glory. Those who express themselves cynically about democracy ought sometimes to remember that democracy is the only form of government about which it is possible to be cynical in public while continuing to live in safety under its jurisdiction.

Commentators insist on the failures of democracy and yet tend to assume the survival of democracy as something to be taken for granted. A strong overt commitment to democracy is less than general: indulgent attitudes to certain of the enemies of democracy are frequent. A free press, whose life-span can be no longer than that of the democratic state under which it exists, has on the whole turned its critical attention more closely on the faults of that state than on the forces which threaten it. This is right, of course, if the faults are great and the threat is slight. The faults are great no doubt, though less I believe than in any other form of organized state that we know. Is the threat slight? There are many thoughtful people who do not regard it as slight today, even in Britain, perhaps the most solidly established of all the world's liberal democracies. It is not regarded as slight either in Italy or Germany. If it is significant in other Western countries, under the economic and social stress of the time, is it likely to be less significant in this land, cursed as it is with private armies, and menaced as it is by the appalling situation which these private armies have precipitated in the North?

In our conditions, there are forces at work which tend to turn the normal sturdy sulkiness of the democratic citizen into something rather more disturbing. There are, to begin with, the lingering elusive doubts about the legitimacy of the state itself. The actual denial of that legitimacy is now confined to a very small, but significant, minority of the population, but the effects of past denials are much more widespread, partly in the forms of doubts, disengagements and disparagements about state and Parliament, and partly in ambivalence towards anti-democratic bodies which arrogate to themselves powers rightly belonging to the democratic state.

To speak more plainly: too many people speak and write as if the armed conspiracies known as the IRA have a legitimate or quasi-legitimate, though usually unspecified, role to play in our society. This permeates the language that is used about them and that language in turn reinforces the peculiar kind of authority which they have held, which has done enormous damage, which may seem perhaps at the moment to be on the verge of decomposing but still requires vigilance, plain speaking and determination in combating it.

I know that, in certain circles, it is regarded as somewhat 'paranoid' even to refer to armed conspiracies. It would indeed be paranoid, if these conspiracies did not exist. Unfortunately they do exist: one of them murdered a member of this House last year, and they continue to murder, maim, and intimidate – especially intimidate – people every day in this island. It is paranoid to see armed conspiracies where none exists. What word is there for a failure to see armed conspiracies where they *do* exist and are murdering our neighbours? But of course it is not really a question of a failure to see them, but of an unwillingness to use words that accurately define their nature. We prefer woollier appellations; thus the words 'the Republican movement' are vague, convenient, give no offence to the conspirators, and are in frequent use.

I think it would be fair to say of many – though certainly not all – of those who write and broadcast in this country that they have fallen over the years into a cautiously propitiatory habit of reference towards armed conspiracies within the Republican family.

Members of these conspiracies when apprehended, tried and convicted are generally referred to as 'Republican prisoners', as if they had been jailed for their opinions and not for crimes, up to and including murder. The more spectacular crimes are indeed strongly condemned and the armed conspirators are frequently implored to desist from violence. Such condemnations and such pleas are very often mingled with tributes to various virtues imputed to the conspirators, and a generous attribution of space to all their communiqués and all the hand-outs of the numerous associations whose only significance derives from the consistency of their alignment with the position of one or other wing of the IRA. There is also a disquieting tendency to attach credence, or the appearance of credence, to statements by the propaganda wings of these conspiracies, in spite of the fact that they have lied, and been caught lying, on so many occasions. I would attach only symptomatic importance here to various individual phrases – the use in a newspaper of the word 'execution' to describe an IRA murder, the uttering by a columnist of a 'shout of joy' at the news of the Portlaoise escapes, the placing by a Dublin periodical very recently of inverted commas around the word 'convicted' in relation to a convicted criminal of Republican tendencies, the use by a commentator of the phrase 'subversive organizations, as the Government calls them'. None of these items is of much significance in itself: what is significant is the frequency with which language of this kind is used, the ease with which it is accepted and the widespread equivocal approach to the IRA which this implies. It is rare to find any explicit total rejection of the IRA as having *any* legitimate role in our society; any explicit recognition of the fact that, in a democracy, there is room for only one army, the army responsible to the people through an elected Government and that the citizens should cooperate with the Government in breaking any private army. I put not long ago to the editor of one of our Dublin newspapers the question whether he regarded the IRA as soldiers fighting for Ireland or as murderers. He published my letter but made no answer. From his editorials I would infer that he would regard them as murderers when they kill people in the twenty-six counties but as soldiers when they kill people belonging to certain categories in Northern Ireland. Unfortunately there are quite a few people, in politics as well as journalism, who share that attitude; and give it oblique expression.

Indeed, if I have laid here an emphasis on journalism, it is by no means because I would suggest that journalists are primarily responsible for our present predicament in relation to armed conspiracies. I do not think anything of the sort: I am discussing journalists here because of the specific bearing of this legislation on journalism. I would agree that people coming from a number of other categories – clergy, teachers, businessmen, trade unionists – bear responsibilities in this area no less than those of journalists. I am not indicting journalists as a class, nor am I indicting the general membership of the other categories I have mentioned. I would agree with journalists when they say that the prime responsibilities rest with the politicians. I would be glad to discuss the responsibilities of politicians in this matter, and how I view the distribution of these responsibilities, at another time and place.*
But here, on this Bill, we are concerned with broadcasting, and with the journalistic context of broadcasting.

I believe that our public are now clear-sighted enough about the IRA, that they see its danger generally, detect the falsity of its promises and want nothing to do with it. The IRA's senseless destructive campaign in Northern Ireland has accomplished that much at least. But a certain miasma of glamour about these organizations still lingers in the channels of communication. This is not entirely due to the way in which explicit communication tends to lag behind the intuitive processes through which ordinary citizens reach their conclusions. There are also, as in the question of attitudes to democracy, factors of more widespread application not confined to our island. Just as violence is attracted to the camera, so the camera is attracted to violence; it is a case of love at first sight on both sides. This is of course due not just to the perversity of cameramen or broadcasters, but to the fascination which violence has for so many people – especially for people who can witness or hear about it happening to others from the

*See the following essay, 'Shades of Republicans'.

safety of their own living room. I think that fascination too has diminished for viewers in the Republic, as the violence has come nearer. The news-value of violence in itself confers an authority of a kind on those who can dispense violence and even on those more remotely connected with it. The utterances of Sinn Fein would certainly not attract one-fifth the attention they do if their spokesmen were not rightly felt to be speaking for the gunmen, in spite of their ritual denials that this is so.

These sympathies, half-sympathies and equivocations have their roots in history. This is true, but it is not a reason for not trying to eliminate them – as many European nations have eliminated their equivalents – if we now find them to be noxious to our own lives and to the prospects of our children.

Many people who originally cherished such sympathies have already weighed them and found them altogether wanting, as far as our life now is concerned. Others, perhaps, while not really supporting the armed conspiracies, would concede them a sort of privileged role, sanctified by historic precedent, existing on a plane above normal judgement, and enjoying, if not a legal immunity, a kind of moral immunity for acts which if committed by ordinary citizens would be crimes. This attitude, understandable enough perhaps in the twenties and thirties, seems now, in 1975, surely to have something sickly and retarded about it. In any case, the state has to reject firmly any such concept of historically privileged crime, and this rejection will necessarily be reflected in legislation and regulations affecting the state broadcasting system.

This is not because there is any serious danger, at the present time, that material sympathetic to the IRA would cause the citizens of the Republic to engage in widespread violence. The results are more long-term, and therefore all the more appropriate to be guarded against by legislation.

Basically, if the state broadcasting system were in any way to accredit the idea that the IRA is a quasi-legitimate institution, or that it is appropriate for citizens to be neutral as between the democratic state and the armed conspiracies which seek to usurp its functions – and have on occasions actually usurped some of those functions – then that pattern of presentation coming from that source – i.e. a source closely associated with the state itself –

would tend to confuse the citizens, by intensifying the false air of legitimacy with which the IRA has managed to surround itself, and would thereby, under any propitious conditions which may occur, further the criminal purposes of these organizations.

Of no less importance than this is the consideration of the impact of our broadcasting in Northern Ireland, where there exists among the majority a widespread impression – greatly, understandably and most ominously strengthened by certain events of five years ago* – that this state is in some kind of collusion with the IRA. Anything in our broadcasting that would seem to confirm that impression is dangerous to life, both in Northern Ireland and here. In normal circumstances, and I hope in all circumstances likely to arise, it is for the Authority to ensure that a proper balance is kept, through the discharge of its responsibilities under law. But in view of the serious implications of these matters for the state and the people, it is necessary for the state to retain a reserve power of intervention which may never be used, but is there in case of need.

This legislation seeks at one and the same time to retain that reserve power and to ensure that it is not used for purposes other than those for which it is needed.

The actual wording of that reserve power, both in Section 16 (1) and also in the parallel prohibition to the Authority contained in Section 3 (1A) will rightly be carefully scrutinized by the Senate and has already been subjected to some criticism in the press and by broadcasters. It is criticized as being unduly wide, and the objection is understandable. It is fair to point out, however, that wide though it may be, it is far less wide than the power conferred by Section 31 of the existing Act – a power which is without limitation of any kind. I wanted to get rid of this absolute power, so obviously capable of manifold abuse, but I wished the power substituted for it to remain wide in the area where its exercise is justifiable: that of security.

The wording used in these sections closely resembles the wording used in the British Independent Broadcasting Act of 1973 (and similar prescriptions applied to the BBC) which have generally

*The 'Arms Trial' crisis of 1970. See below, 'Shades of Republicans'.

not given much concern to journalists and broadcasters. The wording has, I think, to be reasonably wide if it is to be effective in application to the many unforeseen situations which may arise, to the ever-changing nature of crime and associated forms of disorder, and to the complex relationship of broadcasting to these.

I think it likely that Senators will seek to amend Sections 16 (1) and 3 (1A). I can promise any such Senators that the most careful consideration will be given to their amendments, and that wherever it can be shown that different wording would tend to eliminate possible abuse, without seriously endangering the objective sought in these sections, and which I have sought to explain in my foregoing words, then I will have no hesitation in accepting that different wording. But I don't want, either, to hold out any excessive hopes of major change. That the Government shall retain an adequate reserve power, for security reasons, is a principle which the Government is determined to safeguard, and any amendments seriously weakening that would be resisted.

I am not under the illusion that any restrictive provisions embodied in broadcasting legislation can be 100 per cent effective. The 1960 Act, which in its present form is considerably more sweeping and drastic in its provisions than it will be if these amendments are carried, was yet by no means always successful in restraining the kind of manifestations which it was presumably intended to restrain. Legislation is static: broadcasting fluid and volatile; broadcasters always impatient of curbs and on occasions ingenious in evading them.

Restraints work only in a clumsy, intermittent and painful fashion unless those concerned are themselves convinced of a *need* for some restraints. If of course it were certain that all broadcasters were convinced of such a need and would in all circumstances remain so, then there would be no need for any external legislative restraint. However, this is not likely to be the case. The broadcaster's professional instinct inclines him towards exposure of what is exciting, even sensational, and to regard the possible social effects of such exposure as conjectural and outside his sphere. Instances of active sympathy with the armed conspiracies and desire to promote their cause by propaganda are rare, though not altogether unknown. A kind of neutral professionalism, indifferent to social consequences, is much more widespread and lasting. It is for this reason that the public interest has to be protected. The old legislation, and the amendments to it which I now propose, both aimed to serve that end. If legislation is to serve that end as effectively as possible, broadcasters and other interested citizens should have the opportunity of understanding, not just the nature of the steps the Oireachtas is taking, but the reasons why it judges such steps to be necessary. In this respect I think that the weakness of the old legislation was not just the unrestricted power conferred by Section 31, but the failure to offer reasons why restrictive powers were needed at all. As a result of this it was natural for broadcasters to regard the section in question as a kind of arbitrary big stick which might be brought down on them at any time in any way and for any reason. I do not believe broadcasters generally will like my Sections 3 (1A) and 16 very much better than the old Section 31 but at least they now have some idea – though they may say not yet a clear enough idea – of the category to which the restrictive power is itself restricted.

They will also have had an opportunity of learning the framework of ideas in which the legislation is set and the intent and frame of mind of the Government with regard to it. It is my belief also that when the debate here and in the Dáil is completed they will have a very full idea of the mind of the Oireachtas on these matters. They have also their opportunity both as citizens and experts to influence our debate, and perhaps also the ultimate form of the legislation. Some of their representatives have been in touch with me on this matter and I believe they will also have been in touch with some Senators about amendments which they consider desirable. Any such amendments which Senators may think worthy of adopting and submitting I shall be prepared to study carefully with a view to improving the wording of this Bill, always subject to the safeguarding of its essential substance. It is my greatest hope that this debate may lead to a better understanding between the Government, the rest of the elected representatives of the people, the broadcasting Authority, the executives of RTE and the professional broadcasters generally, with regard to the legislative framework of broadcasting in this country.

The thinking behind a law, as expressed during a debate on a Bill, has to be considered irrelevant by the judges who interpret the law. It will not, however, I think be felt to be altogether irrelevant by those who have to work under that law.

Shades of Republicans

In the course of a statement in the Senate* introducing the Broadcasting Authority (Amendment) Bill I referred to 'the lingering elusive doubts about the legitimacy of the state itself', to 'ambivalence towards anti-democratic bodies which arrogate to themselves powers rightly belonging to the democratic state' and to people who 'speak and write as if the armed conspiracies, known as the IRA, have a legitimate or quasi-legitimate, though usually unspecified, role to play in our society.'

Speaking in the context of the Broadcasting Bill, most of what I had to say in this connection directly concerned journalists and broadcasters.

I added, however: 'I would agree with journalists when they say that the prime responsibilities rest with the politicians. I would be glad to discuss the responsibilities of politicians in this matter, and how I view the distribution of these responsibilities, at another time and place.'

The *Irish Times* has now taken me up on this point and has offered me space to explain what I had in mind. This I now propose to do. When I spoke of the responsibilities of the politicians I had in mind a general amalgam of political attitudes in the Republic, inherited from the past, and affording a kind of cover for IRA activities. And when I spoke of the distribution of these responsibilities I had in mind primarily the relationships of Fianna Fáil ('the Republican Party') to the rest of what is called the Republican movement. Fianna Fáil's responsibility in this matter is the prime factor to be considered, because of the size of

*Reprinted above, 'Broadcasting and Terrorism'.

that party and the duration of its periods of power, because it tended to set the tone, over the last forty years or so, for political discourse in the Republic generally, and because its historical, psychological and rhetorical relationships to the post-Treaty IRA are incomparably closer and deeper than is the case with any other political grouping (except Sinn Fein and the Republican splinters which have recently come off Fianna Fáil itself). These relationships, as they have evolved over the years, are exceedingly complex, and I can hope here to do no more than touch on some of the salient features in them. It will become apparent, I hope, that I am not attempting to indict the Fianna Fáil party for its role in history. Edmund Burke knew no way of indicting a nation, and it would not be much easier to indict such a significant part of a nation as has supported Fianna Fáil. Nor is a courtroom approach to political responsibilities often appropriate, though it has occasionally become so. Generally, in speaking of political responsibilities, it is well to bear in mind the maxim of Karl Marx: 'Men make their own history, but they do not make it in conditions of their own choosing.'

It was quite clear, even before the Anglo-Irish Treaty of 1921, that whatever the outcome in other matters, Ireland would be divided. This was accepted even by the extraordinary politician who was regarded as the leader of the Republican cause, and who founded Fianna Fáil. The minutes of proceedings of the private session of the second Dáil for 22 August 1921 – during the Truce period – record the following:

An tUachtaran [the President, Eamon de Valera] . . . They [i.e. Dáil Eireann] had not the power, and some of them had not the inclination to use force with Ulster. He did not think that policy would be successful. *They would be making the same mistake with that section as England had made with Ireland* [writer's italics]. He would not be responsible for such a policy. . . . For his part, if the Republic were recognised, he would be in favour of giving each county power to vote itself out of the Republic if it so wishes.

(Incidentally this statement, though made in 1921, was not officially published until 1972. The wisdom of the approach recommended at the time the statement was originally made should have shone out at the date of the publication, but in fact was hardly noted.) There ensued the Treaty, the Treaty debates – in which, as is well known, the question of Partition received little discussion – the Civil War and the establishment of the Free State.

Before the Treaty Mr de Valera had accepted some form of partition as inevitable. During the Treaty controversy, Mr de Valera's alternative to the Treaty – Document No. 2 – did not differ materially from the Treaty in relation to partition. But after the Civil War he and his defeated followers had a very obvious political temptation: *to blame partition on the Treaty*. They had laid down their arms, but they were still denying the legitimacy of the new State. The formal grounds for denial – differences between the Treaty and Document No. 2, together with the question of the rights of plenipotentiaries and the circumstances of the dissolution of the second Dáil – could hardly be expected to arouse an electorate in the post Civil War period. But the idea of the 'injustice of partition', as something cravenly accepted by one side and stoutly rejected by the other, was both intelligible and emotive. It was also familiar, being one of the main arguments which Sinn Fein in the days of its unity had used to destroy Redmond and Dillon.

Certain pro-Treaty statements had made the mistake of over-selling the Boundary Commission clause in the Treaty as opening the way to unity, since it was held that the Commission's findings would necessarily lead to the transfer of large tracts of Northern Ireland to the Free State, so that the remainder of the area would cease to be a viable entity. When these hopes collapsed and the Free State Government had to conclude the 'no change' Boundary Agreement in 1925, the Republican Opposition was presented with a powerful opportunity/temptation. There was a legitimate opportunity for any opposition at the time to point out that the Border was unjustly drawn, and that the hopes nourished by pro-Treaty spokesmen for serious boundary revision had proved delusive. The temptation was to go beyond that and try to wrap the general responsibility for partition round the neck of the Government. To that temptation Mr de Valera now succumbed. On 10 December 1925 he said in a speech at a protest meeting in the Dublin Rotunda:

For Republicans there can be no two opinions on that question. We may have to bow our heads for a time to the enforced partition of our country by a foreign Power, but the sanction of our consent that partition can never have.

We deny that any part of our people can give away the sovereignty or alienate any part of this nation or territory. If this generation should be base enough to consent to give them away, the right to win them back remains unimpaired for those to whom the future will bring the opportunity.

There can be few clearer indices of the damage done by the Civil War than the contrast between this emotional appeal and the thoughtful statement of the same leader a little more than four years before in the secret session of the Dáil. Partition, then acknowledged as inevitable, and indeed legitimate in respect of any counties which would wish to 'opt out', was now rejected as utterly illegitimate, and anyone who might consent to it branded as 'base'.

Partition was now established as a potent, though an intermittent, issue in the politics of the twenty-six counties. It was linked ominously with the question of the legitimacy of the state, which Fianna Fáil continued to question for years even after their entry into the Dáil. The first phrase in a declaration by Mr Sean Lemass in 1928 – after entry into the Dáil – is still often recalled:

Fianna Fáil is a slightly constitutional party. We are perhaps open to the definition of a constitutional party, but before anything we are a Republican party. We have adopted the method of political agitation to achieve our end because we believe, in the present circumstances, that method is the best in the interests of the nation and of the Republican movement, and for no other reason. Five years ago the methods we adopted were not the methods we have adopted now. Five years ago we were on the defensive, and perhaps in time we may recoup our strength sufficiently to go on the offensive. Our object is to establish a Republican Government in Ireland. If that can be done by the present methods we have, we will be very pleased, but, if not, we would not confine ourselves to them. [Dáil Eireann, Parliamentary Debates 22:1615.]

A statement with similar implications was made by Mr de Valera himself in the following year.

I still hold that your right to be regarded as the legitimate Government of this country is faulty. You have secured a *de facto* position. Very well. There must be some body in charge to keep order in the community, and by virtue of your *de facto* position you are the only people who are in a position to do it. But as to whether you have come by that position legitimately or not, I say you have not come by that position legitimately. You brought off a *coup d'état* in the summer of 1922. [Dáil Eireann, Parliamentary Debates 28:1398.]

Why was the state not legitimate? Mr de Valera might adduce historical–juridical concepts, like the notion that what happened in 1922, with the support of a majority in the Dáil and in the country was a *coup d'état*, but the most powerful, emotive and intelligible argument available against the legitimacy of the state was the concept of its imperfection: that the whole island of Ireland was the real unit and that a Government elected by the people of the twenty-six counties was not the Government of Ireland and was, therefore, illegitimate. Fianna Fáil did not explicitly endorse this line of argument – it had good reason not to, as it aspired to power in the twenty-six counties – but the trend of its rhetoric, before it achieved power, was in that direction. Furthermore, even the explicit statements of its leaders had logical implications of an ominous character. According to Mr De Valera's Rotunda utterance of 1925, the right to win Northern Ireland back 'remains unimpaired for those to whom the future will bring the opportunity'. Since he and his principal supporters cast doubt on the legitimacy of the twenty-six-county state it seemed to follow rather clearly that that state would have no right to restrain any young men who might think that they saw the opportunity to exercise their unimpaired right to win back Northern Ireland.

Fianna Fáil is a party of many aspects: this was one aspect and it would be easy to dismiss it as merely the rhetoric of a transient phase in the history of the party. Unfortunately, as time was to show, there was more to it than that.

Certainly, as Fianna Fáil approached power, it was less concerned to assert rights over the North than to reassure the electorate that it had no dangerous intentions in the matter. Mr de Valera's pre-election statement on 11 February 1932 sought a mandate in relation to the oath, land annuities and other payments, various economic matters and the encouragement of the Irish language but made no reference to the North other than what might be contained in the cryptic statement: 'We pledge ourselves, that, if elected in a majority, we shall not in the field of international relations exceed the mandate here asked for without again consulting the people.'

In office, and questioned in the Dáil about his policy on partition Mr de Valera replied as follows: 'The only policy for abolishing partition that I can see is for us, in this part of Ireland, to use such freedom as we can secure to get for the people in this part of Ireland such conditions as will make the people in the other part of Ireland wish to belong to this part' (1 March 1933).

This was of course about as far a cry from his irredentist pledge of 1925 as that had been from his acceptance of partition in 1921 and it was in substance though not in form a return to the 1921 position. In fact Mr de Valera was again on top and the time for irredentist rhetoric and questioning the legitimacy of the state had been in the period of Opposition. As far as the legitimacy of the State was concerned, Mr de Valera set that right, to his own satisfaction, by the Constitution of 1937. Articles 2 and 3 of the Constitution served the purpose, I believe, not so much of 'laying claim to the North' – though unfortunately they looked like that to the North – as of demonstrating the legitimacy of the state ruled over by Mr de Valera – as distinct from what was in all essentials the same state when ruled over by Mr Cosgrave. This was done by language intended to show that Mr de Valera's state, though identical in territory with Mr Cosgrave's, had not been a consenting party to that state of affairs, the guilt for which therefore did not taint its legitimacy. Paradoxically, the effect of this language was to establish the present-day fact that 'Ireland', in law, consists of twenty-six counties. The refinement of this conception did not impress Republicans outside the Fianna Fáil fold. As for Mr de Valera's followers, they hardly needed so subtle a reassurance. For them the state was legitimate since Fianna Fáil was in charge of it.

Mr de Valera did not again resume a crusading posture about Northern Ireland until he fell from office in 1948 and went on a world tour with Mr Aiken to arouse the conscience of the world on the matter.

The inter-party Government of that day, which included a Republican component led by Mr Sean McBride, joined for a time with Fianna Fáil in a burst of irredentist rhetoric and propaganda. The present writer, as a civil servant in the Department of Foreign Affairs, was involved in this and learned from it, by experience, the hollowness of 'anti-partition'. Then Fianna Fáil came back and the whole thing was dropped once more. Later, after the departure from the active scene of Mr de Valera, Mr Lemass in the mid-1960s tried a policy of *rapprochement* with the Northern authorities which might perhaps have worked if it could have been initiated much earlier and maintained steadily – if in fact Mr de Valera's approach of 1921 could have been maintained. The policy might even have begun to work in 1965 but for the unfortunate and unavoidable fact that the following year was 1966. That was a year in which the ghosts of 1916 had to walk and the traditional rhetoric had to be heard again. The IRA benefited from this and so did the extreme loyalists in the North. The stage began to be set.

A political leader like Mr de Valera may adjust his rhetoric, and indeed his professed opinions, to the needs of a given situation and get his party to follow him. However, the rhetoric so firmly based in the traditions of the foundation years of the party has a life of its own, usually divorced from practice but having a potential contingent bearing on practice. Fianna Fáil Governments have often dealt ruthlessly with the IRA, but the inmost sentiments of many of its followers still yearn towards them. Late on the night of the marathon debate in May 1970, following the dismissal or resignation of Messrs Blaney, Haughey, O'Morain and Boland, a large group of Fianna Fáil deputies at Leinster House was to be heard singing. These deputies were supporters of Mr Lynch, and about to vote confidence in him. The song they were singing was 'The Bould Fenian Men'. They were about to shove into outer darkness the nearest approximations they possessed to 'Bould Fenian Men' but the song came to their lips nonetheless, apparently without any feeling of incongruity. The practical world was a world of party discipline in which you had to fire Republicans if they were caught doing something that might damage the party. The world of sentiment, of conviviality and song was another matter.

Of course Fianna Fáil was not altogether alone in fostering a rhetorical and sentimental tradition, and a blurring of realities, which helped to maintain for the IRA – alias 'the Republican movement' – the status of a half-acknowledged though submerged institution, still trailing clouds of romantic legitimacy. Before Fianna Fáil was, the ballads were, and the ballads may still be sung when Fianna Fáil is gone: the 'rhetorical and sentimental tradition' cannot just be blamed on Fianna Fáil; rather that tradition is one of Fianna Fáil's begetters; the other being a cold, intelligent and ruthless pragmatism. Nor does the blurring of realities begin with Fianna Fáil. The old Irish Parliamentary Party steadfastly refused, for as long as ever it could, to take into clear focus the solid fact of Ulster Protestant refusal to be incorporated in an Irish state detached from Britain. The old Sinn Fein inherited and magnified that refusal. Ulster Protestant Unionists were Britain's dupes or pawns – and of course at the same time staunch level-headed people who very soon, when they had realized the errors of their ways – in which they might be helped by a good shove – would make a tremendous contribution to a united Ireland. Only England's interference stood in the way of this desirable, and otherwise imminent consummation. This mess of unexamined notions spread at one time well beyond the boundaries of the Fianna Fáil/Republican moral community. And of course down in the soggy depths of that mess is the justification for the post-Treaty IRA: if the only thing that keeps Ireland from being united is British force, then it is legitimate for Ireland to use force to put the British out. And in practice, granted the relative strengths of the two countries, the only force available is guerrilla force.

A mess of crazy premises can nonetheless have a corollary that logically follows from these premises. In this case, the corollary of the mess was the IRA as a force to be publicly disavowed, but tacitly condoned in relation to Northern anti-British operations.

In practice, from 1932 to 1969, no one in any position of responsibility in Fianna Fáil showed any patience with attempts to put into practice what might be the logical consequences of the foolish premises which they professed to hold so dear. In practice, as distinct from sentiment, Fianna Fáil has proved at critical moments in our history the most effective enemy of the IRA.

Thus in 1927 Mr de Valera and his followers went through a process which from the point of view both of the pro-Treaty opponents and the former IRA allies, was indistinguishable from the taking of that Oath,* which was the most powerful of the symbols over which the Civil War had been fought. This act, indefensible in terms of the rhetoric of those who executed it, was nonetheless (or *ipso facto* if you prefer) an act of high political wisdom, and a major contribution to political democracy in our country. Another great contribution came five years later when W. T. Cosgrave's Government set the so-far-unmatched example of a peaceful transfer of power by leaders who had won a civil war to leaders who had lost it. (This unique transaction has recently been the subject of a monograph by an American political scientist Frank Munger, *The Legitimacy of Opposition: The Change of Government in Ireland in 1932* (London/Beverly Hills, 1975).) Again, during the war years, Mr de Valera, coldly turning his back on the 'England's difficulty is Ireland's opportunity' tradition, undertook that Irish soil would not be used as a base for attack on England, and honoured that undertaking with the most implacable severity, through internment and through execution of Republicans who favoured taking the long-awaited 'opportunity'. Again, when a revived IRA directed a campaign against the North in the late 1950s, Mr de Valera's successor, Seán Lemass put it down, again using internment, without hesitation, and with obvious indifference to any contradiction between this course of action and, say, Mr de Valera's old Rotunda prophesyings, the annual rededications of Bodenstown, or indeed the slightness of his own constitutionalism in the earlier days.

'*Tout commence en mystique, et finit en politique*', wrote Charles Péguy. Mr Lemass may not have given much thought to Péguy but he understood very well the concept of a transition from nationalist *mystique* to a politics of common sense and coexistence, and deserves great credit for doing his best to speed that transition on.

There were two great catches in all this, and in these catches that party is now caught.

The first catch was, and is, that the *mystique*, albeit in a somewhat battered and debased form, remained part of the party's

*To the British Crown.

political stock-in-trade, much cherished by the rank and file as their distinguishing badge of merit. They like, on appropriate times and occasions, to see themselves as chosen ones, Soldiers of Destiny, Legion of the Rearguard, more Irish and better Irish than the rest of the people. This concept of a national élite stands in an uneasy relation to the similar image of itself held by the IRA. As true descendants of the Republican side in the Civil War the IRA has to look more plausible, *even to Fianna Fáil*, than Fianna Fáil does. This entails a sneaking respect for the IRA, the only category of the population not deemed to be less truly Irish than Fianna Fáil. 'The boys' might have to be disciplined from time to time, but your heart went out to them all the same. Especially when Fianna Fáil was out of office.

The second catch, now gripping hard, is that, given this unusually strong tension in the party between *mystique* and pragmatic politics, the authority of a strong leader is required to prevent the party lapsing into incoherence or worse. Mr de Valera possessed that authority. So did Mr Lemass. In each case, this authority did not depend on holding the office of Taoiseach. Being personal to the leaders concerned, and derived from the history of their movement and party, it held good equally in Opposition as in Government. Under such iron leadership, in office and out, the practical primacy of political common sense over sentiment and *mystique* could be steadily maintained.

But authority of this kind was not easily transmitted from the veterans to the new generation which grew under their formidable shadow. The first generation of Fianna Fáil leaders had won power early and held it long. In recruiting the younger people who would eventually succeed them they looked – as other parties in a similar position have done – not for qualities that would make for good leadership in the future, but for qualities making for good followership in the present. In Fianna Fáil's peculiar position, they wanted people who would say the usual things and do what they were told, even when what they were told to do appeared to conflict with the usual things they were expected to say. The people who conformed to these requirements made excellent followers, the voting strength of a disciplined party. But when, in due course of time, they were themselves called on to lead, the qualities which had made for their selection as followers did not stand them in good stead. Some of them, who believed the things they had all been saying, actually believed also that, when in power, they should act on what they had been saying, rather than follow the pattern of what they had been doing, in the time when they were capably led. Mr Kevin Boland's speech in the notable debate of May 1970 is a museum-piece of this kind.* He was clearly a prisoner of the rhetoric of Fianna Fáil's past, which was also the rhetoric of the men whom his father† had put in jail for acting on that rhetoric.

Others tried to do what their elders would have done but – through no fault of their own – could have nothing like the same assurance of being followed. We can be sure that Mr Lynch sincerely wished to continue consistently the pragmatic policies of Mr Lemass, the primacy of *politique* over *mystique*. He has been less than fully successful in doing so.

One cannot easily imagine either Mr de Valera or Mr Lemass allowing any of his ministers anything like so free a hand in relation to matter of major national policy as Messrs Haughey and Blaney‡ are known to have exercised in the fateful period from September 1969 to May 1971. Nor can one imagine Mr de Valera or Mr Lemass waiting for a public warning from the leader of the Opposition before dismissing the ministers in question. And least of all can one imagine either of those former leaders reinstating on his front benches a former minister whom he had dismissed, especially not a former Minister for Finance under whom moneys voted for one purpose were found by the Public Accounts Committee of the Dáil to have been expended for another purpose, largely unknown to this day, and presumably unknown at the time to the then Taoiseach who has now restored, as far as is within his power, his enterprising and reticent ex-minister.

The Haughey restoration is generally regarded as due to a kind of Republican rebellion inside Fianna Fáil, a recrudescence of the *mystique*. It comes, ironically, at a time when that *mystique*,

*A Fianna Fáil minister who resigned in May 1970 in protest at the dismissal of two other Fianna Fáil ministers for suspected complicity in arms transactions (for which they were then tried and acquitted).

†Gerald Boland, formerly Minister for Justice.

‡The two dismissed Fianna Fáil Ministers referred to in the first footnote above.

as a result of its consequences over the past five years, is discredited to an unprecedented extent outside the Fianna Fáil community – as to some extent also, I think, within that community.

Fianna Fáil, unlike either of the other democratic parties, shared a particular past with the predecessors of the present IRA, together with whom they had defied in arms the verdict of the majority of the people. Fianna Fáil broke with that past in practice, but never entirely in sentiment or rhetoric. Would the IRA have survived, in particular would it have developed a new and virulent strain, if the common culture which it precariously shared with that party had not sustained its pride, its morale, and its sense of historical justification, and preserved it from isolation, even while occasionally restraining or punishing it? We cannot be sure of the answer, but it seems reasonably clear that without that common culture the IRA would have been considerably less dangerous, and in particular the new and virulent strain – the Provisionals – might not have evolved. The new strain of IRA which developed in 1969 was the product not *just* of the situation in the North – which could and should have developed peacefully after September 1969 – but *also* of that situation as envisaged and acted on by the tradition in the Republic which spans Fianna Fáil and the rest of the Republican movement, and which saw in that situation the opportunity prophesied by Mr de Valera in the Rotunda for a generation whose hour would be deemed to have struck.

Mr de Valera would certainly not have deemed it to have struck in 1969. Others did, with horrible consequences. Fianna Fáil's *mystique* got out of control in 1969–70. We do not yet fully know just how much out of control it got, but we know something of the damage that was done. Mr Blaney told the Dáil on 1 December 1972:

Not only did circumstances bring the freedom fighters into existence but so did the promised support of help, not just by me but by a lot of other people as well. The blame lies on me and a whole lot of others, who helped to bring into existence shortly after those who are now condemned as terrorists, murderers – the gunmen of the Provisional IRA. [*Dáil Debates*, vol. 264, col. 668.]

Elsewhere in the same speech (col. 666) Mr Blaney made it clear that the 'whole lot of people' whom he mentioned included 'a large number of most influential members of this House'.

Mr Blaney's statement stands on the record of the Dáil without contradiction from any of his former associates in Fianna Fáil.

Part of the damage done during that period of collusion is tragically obvious: the letting loose of the Provisional IRA in Northern Ireland. The damage done in the Republic is more insidious: damage done to the fabric of our institutions, through the example set in high places of collusion with an armed conspiracy. The damage, fortunately, was not irreparable, but it has taken time to repair it.

It used to be said: 'Yes, it was bad all right but when Jack found out about it, he put his foot down.' Unfortunately he now seems to have forgotten what it was he found out, and to have taken his foot up again.

I don't know how anyone with a clear recollection of the Arms Trial period can look at a picture of Fianna Fáil's new front bench without a sense of revulsion. There is Mr Gibbons who swore that Mr Haughey's sworn testimony was untrue. There is Mr Haughey, who swore that Mr Gibbons's sworn testimony was untrue. There is Mr Lynch who dismissed Mr Haughey, put him on trial, and said he was not satisfied with the verdict that acquitted him. And look again at Mr Haughey who once publicly indicated that resignation was the 'honourable course' for the leader at whose hands he has now accepted reappointment. . . .

The inner conflict between *politique* and *mystique* has left both elements looking remarkably sick.

I said at the outset that there was no way of indicting such an entity as Fianna Fáil. Nor is there. One can, however, note symptoms of serious illness in a political organism. These symptoms declared themselves in Fianna Fáil in 1969. After 1970 they seemed to be clearing up. They are plainly present again in the picture of the new Front Bench, and I think the public discerns them. The public may not remember the details of the crisis of 1970, but at the least it does remember that there was at that time 'some business with the IRA'. A public which most decidedly wants *no* business with the IRA is likely to feel that there is something a little bit wrong with that picture.*

---

*I was wrong there (1977).

Nation Shall Speak Peace Unto Nation Among Other Things

It is oddly appropriate that this Symposium, concerned with a major breakthrough in the possibilities of broadcasting, should be held here in Dublin. For it has been held that it was here in Dublin that broadcasting began, at precisely 5.30 pm on Tuesday 25 April 1916. Professor Marshall McLuhan, in the radio section of *Understanding Media*, points out that whereas before that date wireless had already been used on ships as ship-to-shore 'telegraph', the innovation in the case of this Dublin transmission was that it was intended not to make a point-to-point message, but as a diffuse *broadcast*, intended to carry a message of general significance to anyone who could hear it – in practice to ships' wireless operators, and, hopefully, through some of these to the American press and people. Professor McLuhan therefore terms this 'the first radio broadcast'.

The historian of Irish broadcasting, the late Maurice Gorham, is somewhat more cautious in his claims for this innovative event, saying: 'This was not broadcasting as we know it, for wireless telephony was not yet available and Morse messages were all that could be sent out. But it was news by wireless, not aimed at any known receiver but sent out broadcast, and that was a new idea in 1916.' Even when we have noted that the message was in Morse, it still does seem to have been the first *broadcast*. The equipment used was a 1½ kilowatt ship's transmitter in the Irish School of Wireless Telegraphy over a fancy-goods warehouse at the corner of Abbey Street and O'Connell Street just across the road from

Keynote address by the author, then Minister for Posts and Telegraphs in the Republic of Ireland, to the Dublin Symposium on Direct Satellite Broadcasting organized by the European Space Agency and the European Broadcasting Union, 23 May 1977.

the General Post Office, both buildings being then held by the Irish insurgents of Easter Week, 1916. The world's first radio news-bulletin was composed by James Connolly, the officer commanding the rebel troops in Dublin.

Please do not misunderstand me. I am not to be taken as swelling with chauvinistic pride as I recall the national associations of this primal event in the history of broadcasting. Even if I were temperamentally inclined to be thus carried away, which I am not, there are clear reasons why it would be inappropriate for me, addressing you, to dwell on this event with unmitigated complacency. I am a minister in a sovereign state, having responsibility to see that domestic laws and international agreements regarding broadcasting are respected: you are a distinguished gathering of people concerned to see that space and the airwaves are used in peaceful and orderly ways. Seen strictly in terms of these responsibilities and concerns, which join us here today, that first broadcast was frankly deplorable.

It was of course illegal, both under the domestic laws of the state in which it occurred, and under the international radio regulations then governing wireless telegraphy. It was also war propaganda, the transmission of words to win support for violent action. And like most war propaganda it was designedly inaccurate and misleading. Yet, accompanied as it was by all these regrettable characteristics, it *was* the first broadcast. . . .

The painful conclusion is, I think, inescapable. Broadcasting was conceived in sin. It is a child of wrath. There is no knowing what it may not get up to.

Especially there is no way of knowing what it may not get up to when its potential is suddenly enormously extended, as by the coming of direct satellite broadcasting.

For those who feel like that, as many do, it is natural to contemplate that advent in fear and trembling. It is in something of that frame of mind, I think, that man ought to contemplate *any* extension of his own powers, knowing what he has done with such extensions in the past. We are not really afraid of broadcasting – that is only shorthand – we are afraid of what we may do to ourselves and to one another *with* broadcasting. In the light of some of the things we have done with the printing press, with the internal combustion engine, with the aeroplane, with the chemicals industry, with nuclear fission, fear of any more power in human hands is legitimate and to some extent salutary. Nor, as I have partly indicated, is the history of broadcasting itself entirely reassuring.

If prudent people with no axe to grind can have such reservations it is not surprising that so many of the great axe-grinders, the rulers of states, should be even more reserved. Rulers tend to be acutely conscious of the subversive possibilities of broadcasting, its use as 'a technique of unsettlement', as Auden wrote of Freud's method. And because rulers are sensitive about this, so what we call the international community – which today is hardly more than an ambiguous and unstable consensus among rulers of sovereign states – is sensitive about it too. Such sensitivity is reflected in the recorded proceedings of the Satellite Broadcasting Conference held in Geneva in January–February of this year. It is even more strongly reflected in the recorded proceedings of the United Nations Legal Committee on the Peaceful Uses of Outer Space.

Dr Kaltenecker, of the European Space Agency, in his very valuable overview of the work of the United Nations on the subject which concerns us here this morning, identifies two opposing concepts in the great international debate.

The first of these concepts stresses the principle of prior consent – that is, that satellite broadcasting should not be directed at the territory and population of any state without the prior consent of the Government of that state.

The second concept is that the principle of prior consent is not acceptable because it runs counter to the principles of the free flow of information and the freedom of exchange of ideas.

It is around these two concepts that I should like the remainder of my remarks to revolve. They may seem sometimes to turn at a considerable distance, but I pray that they will remain at the rhetorical equivalent of the satellite's geostationary orbit, within the limits which enhance communication rather than impede it.

For convenience, I shall refer to the first concept as the 'states' rights' concept and the second as the 'free flow' concept. Broadly, the 'states' rights' people are preoccupied with the destructive or subversive possibilities of direct satellite broadcasting, while the 'free flow' people emphasize the liberating

possibilities of this development. It is also important to be aware
of the extent to which political concepts like 'states' rights' and
'free flow' are code-words for the commercial realities which
underlie *Western* broadcasting systems. Politics is of course the
reality, and advertising the remote and alien concept, to *Eastern*
systems.

Advertising can be portrayed as exploitative, a licence to print
money. It can also be seen as subversive, an attempt to instil the
values of a consumer society.

The heightened expectations created by commercial television
can, of course, be politically unsettling in a society with widely
differing levels of wealth.

This may be one of the reasons for the reluctance of South
Africa to embark on television. 'The Lucy Show' may have more
far-reaching effects than Marxism–Leninism. The increasing
international spread of television may increasingly reveal the
wide disparities in a world society.

So far, of course, its audience has merely defined a group sufficiently affluent to afford a TV set.

The 'free flow of thought's commercial counterpart is that
advertisers are the broadcasters most keenly concerned with
whether the audience is switched to their channel.

This is an element which many national systems of broadcasting
find necessary to introduce. To put it at its lowest, how can a
public finance-system dedicated to reducing frivolous demands on
the public purse properly evaluate the amount the public is
willing to spend on entertainment?

Of course, what looks 'subversive' from one point of view looks
'liberating' from another. The primal broadcast from O'Connell
Street can be seen in either aspect.

It is possible that both those who fear the destructive, and those
who hail the liberating, possibilities of extended international
broadcasting are exciting themselves unduly. There can be no
certainty about this. Man is wonderfully ingenious at transmitting
words and images, but still profoundly ignorant about what
happens when these words and images impinge upon his own
nerves and mind. Reading of various treatises and articles on
such subjects as 'Violence and the Media' has put me in mind of
J. D. Beresford's little fable, *The Hampdenshire Wonder*. A little

boy, a four-year-old infant prodigy, puzzles his teachers with his questions about God. The local vicar, a scholar, gives the boy the run of his library. The boy steadily ploughs his way through this vast theological collection, and finally tells the vicar that he has read it all. 'Well,' asks the vicar, 'is there a God then?' The little boy tips his cap respectfully, replies 'No data' and departs.

If we are essentially in a 'no data' situation about such subjects as the relation of the media to violence, this does not mean we can assume they may not be either increasing or reducing the general level of violence. The extent and intensity of public interest in broadcasting – and not least in broadcasting related to violence – make it reasonable to assume that it must be changing people's attitudes, and therefore their behaviour, in some ways. The commercial model is after all entirely based on this presumption. For the rest we have no alternative for the moment but to make the best guesses we can and improve them by trial and error.

One of the most thought-provoking guessers in this domain is the writer I quoted at the outset, Marshall McLuhan. Professor McLuhan is perhaps the most confident evangelist of the 'free flow' school. For him, direct satellite broadcasting, with the specific dramatic extension which it brings to television, has to be welcomed wholeheartedly. Within his system of ideas, direct satellite broadcasting is not merely an important stage in the development of the global village – it is a *benign* stage in that development. Television, for him and his disciples, is a 'cool' medium. 'It involves us in moving depth', he explains, 'but it does not excite, agitate or arouse.'

Well, I wonder. Indeed I have some cause to wonder. Seven years ago, almost to the day, I was an involuntary participant in a little experiment which appears to invalidate the McLuhan thesis, at least in its absolute form. This occurred in Belfast where I took part in a televised panel discussion which included the Reverend Ian Paisley, a dynamic local guru. Early in the show Mr Paisley took umbrage – to which indeed he is somewhat addicted – and left the studio. By the time the other participants, including myself, were ready to leave, a small crowd of Mr Paisley's admirers had gathered in the street outside the broadcasting station. One glance at that crowd was enough to show that its members had not read Marshall McLuhan. They did not know that television was a cool medium. They were excited, agitated, aroused. As we left that station, with the help of the police, we had occasion to regret that we had not taken part in a radio programme rather than a televised one. Radio may be a hot medium, but at least an unpopular radio broadcaster is not recognizable at sight. In that respect, and for the person of the broadcaster, television can be the hotter medium of the two.

The vastly wider diffusion of television is not likely to be attended just by the wholly benign effects announced by Mc-Luhan, or the more enthusiastic advocates of 'free flow'. The global village to be called into being by what he calls 'the unifying synaesthetic force' of television is a Utopia. Bangladesh will not feel like Beverly Hills, or think like it, just because it watches the same television programmes. People can watch the same programmes with quite different feelings, and even different perceptions. Indeed the extent to which broadcasting 'links' people, whether in different countries, or inside the same country, can be exaggerated, not only by prophets like McLuhan, but by more sober thinkers. Thus, it is stated in the United Kingdom's Annan Report that broadcasting welds society together: 'It links people, gives the mass audience common topics of conversation, makes them realize that, in experiencing similar emotions, they all belong to the same nation.' 'Common topics of conversation' is right – and not without importance – but I have some doubts about the 'similar emotions'. In the most dangerous cases of fragmentation, people can watch the same programme, in the same city, with diametrically opposite emotional responses. Television may bond people more closely together, if they already feel bonded, but if they don't feel that way it cannot be safely assumed that television is bonding them together.

In the debate between the two concepts I am disposed to allow the 'free flow' side the benefit of the doubt in any given instance, but I think the existence of very large doubts has to be recognized and that the fears and reservations of the restrictionists are not necessarily entirely unwarranted. It is true that the multiplicity of such objections is oppressive. Our co-Chairman Sir Charles Curran summarizes them in his introduction to the Special Number of the EBU *Review*:

Copyright owners seek to protect their putative rights, almost unaware that their assertions could frustrate the whole development. Cultural and political interests raise objections before there is anything to resist – only fear of what might be. States fortunately situated near the Equator tentatively think about extending their sovereignty vertically without limit in order to claim jurisdiction over orbital positions.

It is a picture that evokes the young Rimbaud's impression of customs officers as 'slashing out the infinite blue frontier with hatchets':

> . . . *Ces soldats du Traité*
> *Tailladent l'azur frontière à coups de hache.*

Yet since there are frontiers on the terrestrial globe, and states and peoples within those frontiers, these phenomena will also be reflected in the infinite blue wherever human beings become active there. And fears about frontiers in space and broadcasting are not necessarily groundless – if that is a proper word to use in such a context. We know that broadcasting can be used to incite to violence because it has been so used. Leaving aside the primal broadcasting event which I have mentioned, the most famous case is that of Hungary, twenty-one years ago.

Many Hungarians have testified that certain regular radio broadcasts from outside that country helped to precipitate the rebellion there, by encouraging the belief that the outside world would come to the aid of the insurgents. The outside world, of course, did nothing of the kind, and the rising was bloodily crushed. It should be particularly noted that the victims of that particular venture in political liberation by means of broadcasting were not the rulers of the country concerned, but the Hungarian people, and especially those amongst that people who were most opposed to their rulers and most in sympathy with the broadcasts.

It is not surprising therefore that some people – including rulers of a certain category of states, but including also people who have no sympathy with those rulers – should be apprehensive about possible political uses of direct satellite broadcasting. It is true that if television was necessarily always a cool and cooling medium it could not be used to incite to political or other violence. As I have said I have some reason to question that assumption. The world would clearly not be a safer place if the superpowers –

or any other powers – were to use the potential of direct satellite broadcasting to attempt to subvert one another's political systems. The danger is real and a danger to humanity at large, irrespective of what one may think of the political systems in question. It is probable that most countries in the world today live under some form of despotism – left, right, or simply crazy. This is a reflection which would be unlikely to win much applause at the General Assembly of the United Nations, but it is true.

It is also true that attempts *from the outside* to change the governments of these countries are not likely to improve matters. Even if successful, they may simply substitute one form of despotism, or one rhetoric of despotism, for another. And to use broadcasting in the service of such attempts is to put people who heed such broadcasting at risk of their lives.

It seems highly desirable therefore that the development of direct satellite broadcasting should be accompanied by conventions against its use for purposes of political propaganda, and in particular against any kind of incitement to political violence.

In speaking of restrictions on incitement to violence, I should perhaps declare a certain interest, both personal and official. As Minister for Posts and Telegraphs in the Republic I have statutory responsibilities in relation to broadcasting. These include responsibility for ensuring that RTE* is not used to broadcast incitement to violence or matter tending to undermine the authority of the state. I have power to issue statutory directions to that end, and I have issued one prohibiting broadcasts of interviews with spokesmen of Provisional IRA and Provisional Sinn Fein.

These statutory powers and that direction are resented by some broadcasters and journalists. My liberal image, I am told by those who can tell such things, is in bits. I am not too worried about that, not being much of a one for images, having indeed some inclination to iconoclasm. But the whole situation has given me seriously to think about restriction and about violence.

And about overspill. You will see that the themes are linked. As you may know, British television spills over into the territory of the Republic. You may ask whether the population is irritated by this intrusion? The answer is: they are if they can't get it.

---

*The Irish Broadcasting Service. See above, 'Broadcasting and Terror'.

Those who are spilled over on don't object. I won't say they wallow in the spill-over but they certainly splash about in it happily enough. I imagine the various spill-overs which are reluctantly contemplated in connection with national satellite programmes may elicit similar responses.

In areas where over-spill does not yet occur, there can be strong demands for it. Satellite broadcasting will inevitably increase over-spill: for example, we know that the beam characteristics of a United Kingdom broadcasting satellite are such that the unavoidable over-spill will cover the whole of Ireland. If and when such a satellite comes into orbit, satisfactory reception of all United Kingdom television programmes broadcast by satellite should therefore become possible in all parts of Ireland, making available to the South and West the kind of multi-channel viewing now available in the North and East. When you visit the South-Western region of this country later this week you may find that the idea of direct satellite broadcasting is of more than academic interest there.

Similarly, the beam characteristics for an Irish broadcasting satellite would give coverage of the whole island of Ireland together with a portion of North-West England and Scotland.

Such developments are far from being immediately imminent, as we all know, but they are not likely to be delayed indefinitely either; your gathering here to discuss this subject is evidence of that. Personally I welcome ordered progress accompanied by an acceptable over-spill. In the broadcasting debate in this country I have opposed the tendency to cultural protectionism which exists among some politicians and intellectuals, though not among the mass of the people whose culture they claim to be protecting. Yet over-spill does create problems. I should like to give an example of one of these. As I have mentioned, RTE is prohibited from broadcasting interviews with spokesmen for the IRA. The British broadcasting stations, which are under no such specific restriction, have broadcast such interviews.

Accordingly, if the faces and words of the IRA Godfathers are wafted into our living-rooms here in Dublin they come to us by courtesy of British broadcasting. The central purpose of the IRA is to 'break the connection' between Ireland and England. Yet it is only in virtue of that connection, in terms of broadcasting, that the IRA has access to the viewing and listening public in Ireland. And it has used that connection to try to win support for its fanatical and lethal anti-British campaign.

This does raise some questions of general interest about the responsibility of broadcasters in these over-spill situations for which direct satellite broadcasts provide the possibility of multiplication and extension.

All broadcasting stations I believe accept, and are required to accept, the principle that they shall not broadcast incitements to crime. The problem is that what may not seem like incitement to crime in the area generating the broadcast may seem just that in the area in which they spill over. It is a problem to which broadcasting stations and broadcasters might give more consideration as we enter the age of direct satellite broadcasts. The specific problem I have raised will be of interest to most of you here this morning only as illustrating the general problem. Of the specific problem I shall say no more than this: I hope my words shall reach those with responsibility for broadcasting in Britain. I would respectfully ask these to consider how they would feel in the corresponding case: that is, if the over-spill from Irish satellite broadcasting into North-West England, Scotland and Northern Ireland were to carry RTE interviews with various categories of subversives into these regions of the United Kingdom?*

The armed conspiracy known as the IRA presents a common threat to the people of Great Britain and of all Ireland. In the considered judgement of the Government of this state, access to broadcasting helps that conspiracy, glamorizes it, promotes its recruiting, enhances its importance in its own eyes and generally encourages it to keep up the killing. Its spokesmen know that it is only through the use of the gun that they have won access to television at all. It is reasonable for them to assume that the more they use the gun the more access they will get and the more progress they will make. It is in this sense that broadcast interviews with such people constitute incitement to crime – not so much incitement of the people at large, most of whom detest the IRA far too much by now to be open to such incitement, but incitement to the killers themselves to keep up the killing, and to

*The then Director-General of the BBC, Sir Charles Curran, who was in the Chair, took mild and courteous exception to this part of my remarks.

potential killers to join the actual ones. The impact of television on the mass public may always be doubtful, but its impact on those who are allowed to broadcast, and who hope to broadcast, admits of no doubt at all.

Its impact on professional broadcasters is also not insignificant. There are some broadcasters whose concept of broadcasting freedom seems to resemble the concept of freedom which was dear to, for example, the feudal aristocracy of Poland and Castile – that is to say, the identification of freedom with the rights and privileges of a caste. This is a widespread human tendency. A powerful Congolese politician whom I once knew used to say: 'The President has no right to push me around. This is a democratic government and as Minister of the Interior I can lock up anyone I want to.'

No broadcaster possesses such powers but some broadcasters do tend to identify freedom of broadcasting with the freedom of the individual broadcaster to broadcast anything he wants to broadcast. Broadcasters in that category will be disposed, I fear, to resent my remarks. But there are many other broadcasters with wider, more complex and more philosophical conceptions of freedom under law in a democratic society. These I hope will be prepared to consider what I have to say in the context of this discussion of extensions in the powers, and therefore in the responsibilities, of broadcasting and broadcasters. These extensions will, I believe, necessitate increasing consultation between those having responsibility for given broadcasts and those affected by the over-spill of such broadcasts.

There is a respectable school of thought which holds that, given the actual state of broadcasting, the extension and multiplication of this medium, through the further use of satellites, is something greatly to be regretted. Their view of the results of extended multi-channel viewing is summarized in the crisp saying 'Fifty times the usual junk'. For many critics of this school the junk in question is not merely useless, but actually noxious, debasing the human mind and psyche with endlessly reiterated violence and drowning ancient cultures in a torrent of trivial admass. This point of view cannot be lightly dismissed, nor is it enough to point in reply to the educational possibilities of direct satellite broadcasting.

The importance of such possibilities has certainly been demonstrated by the remarkable Indian experiment, SITE, which must be of great interest to other countries with comparable problems and opportunities, such as the countries of the Maghreb which are members of your Union. Yet of course terrestrial broadcasting also has important educational achievements to its credit, but these are dwarfed by its enormous use for entertainment. And this will almost certainly also be generally the case with satellite broadcasting. The fact is that people *like* junk; they like, that is, to be amused and entertained. They often don't find the resources of their ancient cultures entertaining enough. In the savannah region of sub-Saharan Africa, men still feed the sacred crocodiles – and rightly so – but when they weary of that, they like to watch very cheap movies made in Bombay about good rajahs and bad rajahs. They can tell the two kinds apart instantly, and the bad rajah is hissed immediately on his first entrance. These poor people do not know it, and they think they are enjoying themselves, but any Western intellectual could tell them instantly that they are in the fell grip of *cultural imperialism*. The fact that it is cultural imperialism emanating *from India* is an irritating and incongruous detail. It *ought* to be the USA and maybe I should have told it that way.

Human nature and human cultures are, I think, much more ingenious, more resilient, more adaptive, and generally less easy to pin down, than seems to be thought by those who most deplore the broadcasting of what they call junk. A real-life horror story will best illustrate my meaning.

I have seen a little girl of six suddenly lunge at her nine-year-old brother's eyes, as if to tear them out. On being denounced by horrified grown-ups she replied cheerfully: 'I saw it on the telly. It's in *King Lear*.' Could you find a better example of the power of television to deprave the young? Well, of course, from the point of view of the puritan critics of television, you *could* find a better example. It is inconvenient that the prime source of this particular depravity should turn out to be a man called Shakespeare, and its immediate source one of those meritorious cultural broadcasts which the puritans think there ought to be more of (and I agree with them on that). It is true that the little girl didn't know it *was* a cultural broadcast. She and her brother had watched it in fascination, quite unaware that they were undergoing an educational experience, which would, of course, have turned them off instantly. But they did know that they were watching a play – and continuing a play. For of course the little girl was not *trying* to tear out her brother's eyes – she was *playing* at doing this, and well her brother knew it. It is true that there have been a few cases in which people have imitated with gruesome literalness some atrocity they saw on television. Some people have therefore assumed that television *caused* them to do these terrible things. In view of the extreme rarity of such events, in proportion to the enormous television audience, it seems safer to assume that the people concerned were mad for other reasons and that television merely suggested the particular form of an atrocity which, in some form, would have happened anyway. The overwhelming majority of people know that a play is a play, and they like playing and plays.

Broadcasting is an extension, and satellite broadcasting a further extension, of the possibilities of play. The most relevant treatise to the theme of this conference may well be J. H. Huizinga's *Homo Ludens* – man playing.

Solemn people, almost by definition, deplore the use of broadcasting as a plaything, and for play-acting. Yet there can be no doubt that this is what humanity mainly wants to use broadcasting for. Nor is this necessarily a bad thing. Solemn people exaggerate the importance of solemnity, and greatly underestimate the importance of play. The impulse to play is at the origin of all the arts. It can have its sinister aspects, as all things human have, but on the whole it can be seen as an expression of the happier, more creative side of human nature. The fact that broadcasting is mostly for play is not therefore to be regretted in itself, though the *quality* of the play may often leave much to be desired. You will not therefore take me as in any way minimizing the importance of your deliberations if I say that the main, though by no means the sole, result of direct satellite broadcasting is likely to be the enlargement of the human playground. The importance of play to human beings is so great and so mysterious as to make this enlargement of the playground a momentous event in human history.

I include, of course, in 'play' the play of imagination and of ideas, the play of encounter and of recognition, the creative and stimulating capacities of broadcasting, the jewels in the junk. Those who are concerned with direct satellite broadcasting will have great opportunities to enlarge the playground in that vital sense.

One possibility is that of an internationally controlled satellite, used to demonstrate the positive and creative possibilities of television, combining entertainment of high quality – which does not mean boring people – with other forms of desirable communication, including perhaps some day the enlargement of the play-dimension through participative broadcasting. It occurs to me as I think of this distinguished gathering here at this Symposium that it represents a community with the financial, technological and cultural resources to provide – if the will to do so is also there – a truly exemplary broadcasting service through the use of a satellite. The cultural riches of the countries represented at this gathering are enormous, both at the present time and in a long perspective of history. Greece and Israel are here, the root-lands of the common heritage of European and American civilization, the Judaeo-Hellenic culture. Italy is here with what that august presence symbolizes in terms of law, of art and of religion. Spain and Portugal, the great discoverers, are here. Britain, France and Germany are here who have led the world in so much, for so long, and in all the arts and sciences. Here we have the Low Countries, matrix of the European Idea. The Scandinavian countries are here, pre-eminent in their lucid concern for international peace and brotherhood. The Arab countries of the Mediterranean are here, who have not only enriched European science and art, but also open the door to wider and different worlds, in Africa and in the East.

What I have in mind is an international satellite, controlled by some kind of consortium of the members of the European Broadcasting Union and the European Space Agency, broadcasting programmes of the highest quality, reflecting the vast heritage of cultures in terms of the realities and the audiences of today. I find that idea an exciting and inspiring one. It may not be immediately practicable but I hope and I believe that it is already a twinkle in some of your eyes.

PART TWO
Herodes Ludens

King Herod Explains

Cast

A SINGER

A PUBLIC RELATIONS OFFICER

HEROD THE GREAT, King of the Jews

A CANDIDATE FOR THE OFFICE OF HIGH PRIEST

MEMBERS OF THE CROWD

Performed at the Gate Theatre Dublin in
1971. Hilton Edwards gave a truly
memorable performance as Herod.

King Herod Explains

Stage and auditorium in darkness

SINGER: Cannot thy hurrying feet
Afford a present for the infant God?
Oh stay. . . .
   [SINGER'S *voice fades. Spotlight on the* PUBLIC RELATIONS
   OFFICER, *a dapper young man in a dinner-jacket*]

PUBLIC RELATIONS OFFICER: His Majesty King Herod
Has graciously agreed to make a personal statement
Arising out of certain grossly unfair imputations
In connection with alleged events of his reign
Published in a tract or pamphlet entitled:
   [*Puts on his spectacles and reads*]
The Gospel According to Matthew.
   [*Replaces spectacles*]
His Majesty understands that this document has been quite
                              widely circulated.
It appears to have been published some time ago,
But has only recently been brought to His Majesty's attention.
His Majesty's object is quite simply to put the record straight.
Not merely by refuting these absurd allegations –
This gross travesty of the facts
About some alleged Massacre of so-called Innocents –
But also about the real and important transactions of his reign,
Some of which remain the object of unnecessary controversy.
   [*A pause*]
Ladies and Gentlemen –
By the way you need not rise.

King Herod has expressed a wish to meet you informally –
[*Reverently*]
Herod the Great,
King of the Jews.

> [*Light on* HEROD *and that part of the stage immediately around him, the rest of the stage remaining in darkness.*
> HEROD *is dressed like Saul, in Rembrandt's 'David playing before Saul'.*
> He should look a little like Saul, and a little like the photographs of Mr Aristotle Onassis. An old man of great intelligence and power, and an air of unreliable benevolence. His throne is large and ornate, and he holds a rather flashy sceptre, which he uses to emphasize his points. He gesticulates freely, with the air of an outsider and a self-made man. Beside* HEROD *is a lay-figure dressed in something approximating to the robes of the High Priest of Jersualem, as described in Exodus*]

HEROD [*quietly*]: You all probably assume that I am guilty ...
I believe my name is a by-word.
Yet are you quite sure what I am guilty of?
[*A pause*]
I am not sure.
[*A pause*]
What you think you know about me is of course like most of
the rest of what you think you know
Quite wrong.
You think it is about the Innocents that I am guilty
From the point of view that it was me or I
Responsible for the famous Massacre of the same.
Well, you're wrong.
[*Stands up, gripping his sceptre. Shouts*]
It wasn't me!
[*Sits down*]
It was a fellow who took my name
Thinking it would do him good.
And just look at the good it did him!
[*A pause*]
Our name is a by-word
[*Sighs*]

I was lucky enough to die before Christ.
He really was the *end*.
  [*A pause*]
Pretending to be King of the Jews!
Out-Heroding Herod!
What a ham!
  [*Rises, speaking with animation, and shaking his sceptre*]
That's it, you know.
That's the real story.
He tried to play *me*
And was howled off the stage!

VOICES FROM THE AUDIENCE : Crucify him! Crucify him!

HEROD [*sits down*] : You were right there.
  The audience is always right.
  You know more than you think you know.
    [*Peers slowly around the audience*]
  You are not such fools as you look.
  It's *me* you want.
    [*Assumes pious demeanour*]
  And I shall always be with you –
    [*Relaxes*]
  Above you, inside you,
  Any preposition you want –
  I'm your man.

FIRST VOICE FROM THE AUDIENCE : Herod for President!

SECOND VOICE : No! *Herod* for President!

THIRD VOICE [*angrily*] : No! No! No! *Herod* for President!

HEROD [*complacently*] : Thank you, gentlemen
  Thank you, one and all.

VOICES : Down with Herod the tyrant!
  Down with Herod the tyrant!

HEROD [*grimly*] : The students are demonstrating –
  Demonstrating their righteousness.
  But they really like me
  Provided I use the appropriate Shibboleth –

H.—F

Which of course I can do
As to the manner born.
    [*A pause*]
The scapegoat you know was a Jewish invention –
    [*A pause*]
Funny that.
    [*A pause*]
And do you know who the *real* scapegoat is?
The scapegoat is not Jesus –
    [*Rises*]
Herod is the scapegoat.
    [*Paces slowly up and down the stage*]
Glory and power in the present
Followed by howls of posthumous execration –
    [*Wheeling to face audience*]
That's what you need, isn't it?
To act bad and feel good about it?
I hope I give you every satisfaction.
Herod for results and then for moral comfort
    [*Rolling the syllables*]
Retrospective de-Her-od-ization!
    [*A pause*]
The Pope condemns Hitler
And the date is 1945
And Hitler is dead.
The Party Congress condemns Stalin
And the date is 1956
And Stalin is dead.
Everybody condemns *me*
Since the date of my death – which, as I now learn,
Took place in the year four
Before Christ.
Before Christ indeed . . .
[*Slowly*] I don't slaughter the Innocents –
The Innocents slaughter me
[*Briskly*] They slay me, they really do.
    [*Sits down*]
[*In a confidential tone*] An old man talking about himself
Is of course a bore.

But I am a cunning old man
And you will find in the end that I am talking about *you*.
Which is the only thing in the world capable of holding your
attention.
Let me tell you, then, something about myself – about yourself.
I am Herod the Great.
Everybody the Great if you like, but anyway Herod.
[*Rapidly*] Not, I repeat not, the gentleman of the same name
who, according to the Christians, killed a lot of children on
the chance they might be Christ, and didn't even catch
Christ.
The man who did that was the *other* Herod –
Not the King of the Jews but the Tetrarch of Galilee.
It was Matthew, calling himself the Evangelist,
The cunning director of Christian propaganda,
Who put the blame on me . . .
   [*A pause*]
Do you know why?
   [*A pause*]
Snobbery, that's why.
Pure snobbery.
It wasn't enough for them that their Messiah
Should be chased by some petty tyrant,
Tracked by the tinpot Tetrarch of Galilee.
Tetrarch Shmetrarch!
No, they wanted to make it a big production –
The full orchestra.
   [*Chest out, head back, eyelids lowered*]
[*Solemnly*] And that required
The King!
The right hand of the Lord of the World!
Herod the Great himself in all his majesty . . .
In full pursuit – of their baby!
   [*Leaps forward and strides across the stage, his hands
   hooked, his expression ferocious, miming the pursuit, then
   relaxes. A pause*]
[*Calmly*] The *King* pursuing *their baby*: that was the point.
And there was another reason:
Their Jesus was really a Galilean,

That is to say a bit of an outsider –
Like, for that matter, myself –
And they wanted him to be a Judaean –
More pukka,
More kosher –
So it wouldn't do for him to be seen to be chased
Not only by a mere Tetrarch but by a Tetrarch of *Galilee* . . .
No, it had to be Bethlehem
In Judaea, the City of David, and the persecutor
Had to be the King of Judaea.
      [*A pause*]
And there was still another reason:
If it was the King of the Jews
Who sought to suppress the child because of a Prophecy,
Why then the King of the Jews –
The last *real* King of the Jews –
Was implicitly recognizing
In this sanguinary manner
The legitimacy of his successor –
Jesus, King of the Jews.
      [*A pause*]
Oh, it was a clever idea, whatever way you like to look at it.
I could have used that Matthew . . .
His stunt worked, I'll never live it down.
As a matter of fact, I was even dead on the date in question.
And it was the other Herod who did it,
Herod the Tetrarch . . .
That man's name was really Antipas
And he was my son . . .
      [*A pause*]
My son whose life I spared.
      [*A pause*]
A certain irony there, don't you think?
You see, I killed my other sons
Aristobulus and Alexander
As well as their mother, the beautiful Mariamne.
I have been much criticized for these actions, posthumously.
At the time, of course, the executions
Were generally held to show firmness and statesmanship

And praised by the historian Nicholas of Damascus –
A very decent fellow who received a pension from my Civil
List.

But you see how everybody misses the point?
My real crime was the crime I did *not* commit.
My real crime was in failing to put to death
The man who took my name and then massacred all those
children.

Look at the mathematics of it:
Antipas was only one man, even if he called himself Herod
Antipas –
Whereas according to the Christians, who admittedly probably
laid it on a bit thick
The children Antipas killed – or, as they said, Herod killed –
numbered four thousand.
Deducting one from four thousand, you will see that what
appeared to be my clemency on that occasion
Caused three thousand, nine hundred and ninety-nine more
deaths than it averted,
Thus bringing the name of Herod into a degree of disrepute
Which could have been avoided by an act of firmness.

A VOICE : Murderer!

HEROD [*severely*] : You should think before you speak,
and you should learn to do your sums.
I killed – all right, I murdered – my son Alexander.
Now, Alexander was a smart boy, much smarter than Antipas –
Which of course is why I found it necessary to murder him.
Now had I spared Alexander, and *he* had been Tetrarch in Galilee
And he had set out to get Christ, why
He would have got Christ.
Right at the start, and no nonsense about it.
So the Christians ought to absolve me for murdering Alexander
And ought to blame me for not having murdered Antipas.
Whereas, of course, what they do is the reverse.
All of which ought to show you the futility and irrelevance
Of attempting to apply moral criteria

To questions of state policy.
[*A pause*]
I was, I really was, a good King.
[*Jeers from the audience*]

HEROD [*rises angrily*]: All right then, let's see!
Give me the names of some good rulers . . .

GENERAL VOICES: Kennedy! Kennedy!

GENERAL VOICES: DeValera! DeValera!

A VOICE: Lincoln!

A VOICE: Michael Collins!

A VOICE: Winston Churchill!

A VOICE: Lyndon Johnson!

HEROD: Very well, I accept all these.
Why may I not be included among them, in the category
of good and wise rulers?

[*Boos and catcalls*]
Murderer! Murderer! Go back to Palestine! There's blood
on your hands!

[*A pause*]

HEROD [*grimly*]: And on whose hands, among those you praise,
is there not blood?

[*A pause*]
Every one of them shed blood, as I did, for reasons of state,
For the preservation of the state,
Which is essential
To ordered human life
And to the very existence of such an audience as yourselves.

A VOICE: You murdered your own family!

HEROD [*smiling*]: You're a sweet lot! So it's all right to murder
people if they don't belong to your own family?

A VOICE: Smart aleck!

ANOTHER VOICE: Jew!
[*A pause*]

HEROD : You have a point there. Or rather half a point.
  I am half Jewish, and I was King of the Jews.
  The Jews, you may be surprised to learn, never cared for me.
  They said I was a Roman,
  And many people, as you may know, feel about Romans
  Very much as many other people feel about Jews, and so on –
  It cuts both ways.
  The Emperor Augustus whom I had the honour to number
                                       among my friends
  Said that he would rather be King Herod's pig than be his son –
  Which must be understood as a fairly blunt allusion
  To the Mosaic prescription against the eating of the flesh of
                                       swine,
  And also to the painful domestic circumstances
                          about which I have told you.

    [*A pause*]
  Now Augustus meant no harm by this rough pleasantry.
  He could no more be anti-semitic
  Than I could be anti-Roman.
  We were both above that sort of thing.
  We were both statesmen.
  It was one statesman talking about another statesman,
  With appreciation and a certain salutary cynicism.
  See the difference between a ruler of men
  And men like yourselves who are born to be ruled!
  You thought it was especially wrong of me to murder members
                                       of my family,
  And then you attacked me for being a Jew.
  Now, as far as the Emperor was concerned, the people
  Whom I might legitimately murder
  Were Jews, because I was King of the Jews,
  And especially Jewish members of my own family
  Because these were obviously the most dangerous Jews
  To the King of the Jews.
  That is why Augustus made his little joke
  Associating infanticide with pork.
  But if I had killed a Roman –
  That would not have been material for a Jewish joke
  But for a Roman holiday.

That is to say for a butchery,
Presented under the polite title of intervention,
Massacre and mayhem on a scale far exceeding the sober limits
Of a modest murder in the bosom of the family.
    [*Sits down*]
Fortunately Augustus and I understood one another
As men do who understand politics.
Our situations were different, of course.
He had the good fortune to govern Romans
Who were people in many ways resembling the British
Whose morality consisted in not running away . . .

ENGLISH VOICE: Bravo!

HEROD: In attending divine service on appropriate occasions,
In not being caught red-handed
In any piece of dishonesty for which a plausible explanation
                                          could not be devised,
    And above all in keeping a straight face.

ENGLISH VOICE: Shame!

HEROD: The last was called *Gravitas*, Augustus was good at it
And the Romans were excellent political material.
I on the other hand had to deal with Jews . . .
    [*He buries his face in his hands. The light on him
    fades and picks up the lay-figure in the priest's robes
    beside his throne*]
HEROD'S VOICE: Can you imagine what it is like to be among
                                          people
Who really believe in God?
    [*A pause*]
No, but *really*?
    [*A pause. Light on* HEROD *again*]
Oh, they didn't all believe in God, thank God.
Quite a lot of them were decent slobs like yourselves,
Who kept the Sabbath, or as you would put it
Went to Mass on Sundays.
Saturday, Sunday, what's the odds?
They were people who would go along,
Quiet people,

Morally unpretentious people.
I gave them a perfectly gorgeous Temple
And I also gave them a Hippodrome
Which is a sort of racecourse
Complete with bars and other amenities
Suited to the tastes of that time.
Sporting men liked me: I was President of the Olympic Games.
I gave my people full employment building the Temple
And the Hippodrome
And also the great port of Caesarea,
Named after my patron and friend
Caesar Augustus.
I planted the balsam groves of Jericho,
Famous throughout the ancient world.
At the same time I managed to keep down the taxes,
Mainly because of my friendship with
Caesar Augustus.
I gave them internal peace
Enforced by troops whom my
               imbecile critics have described as mercenaries . . .
Mercenaries!
As if there were some kind of troops that you could get for free!
And I won for them also the great blessing
Of peace with other lands and most especially
Peace with the Roman power.
I suppose you think that was easy?
My successors found out how easy it was . . .
By the time they were through all that was left of the Temple
Was the Wailing Wall.
      [*Rises with an air of authority*]
My main achievements were in the field of diplomacy.
I think I can claim the honour
Of being the most successful diplomatist who ever lived.
Yes, I can substantiate that.
      [*Walking up and down*]
I lived, you see, in exceptionally dangerous times.
It was the time of the Roman civil wars . . .
When Julius Caesar was killed, the party that was strongest in
                              my part of the world

Was the party of the conspirators.
The Republican Party.
So I became a Republican.
I wasn't yet a King, so that was all right.
The man I mostly had to deal with was a fellow called Cassius –
You must have read about him in Shakespeare?
Well frankly, I laughed when
I read Shakespeare's *Julius Caesar.*
He makes Cassius a lively, temperamental fellow,
Rather witty.
Well, that was Shakespeare not Cassius.
Cassius was a bore.
    [*A pause*]
It is true of course that as well as being a bore
Cassius was a murderer.
You might have thought that would have formed a bond
                                                                between us?

But no.
You see there are murderers and murderers –
Modest murderers and pretentious murderers.
I was one of the modest ones.
Cassius was the other kind –
The boring kind.
At a time when we might have been talking
About industry and commerce, agriculture, finance and defence –
All profitable subjects, especially at that time defence –
Cassius would do nothing but drone on about Julius Caesar.
It was depressing and alarming.
Depressing because the more he went on
About the tyranny of Julius and the virtues of Cassius
The more it became apparent to me how unlucky the Romans
                                                                were

In losing Julius and acquiring Cassius.
I wasn't really worried about the Romans,
But personally I was stuck with Cassius
When what I needed was Julius.
That was the depressing part but the alarming thing was this:
[*Rapidly*] It became apparent to me that in
                                    going on all this time about the

wickedness of Julius and about how ethical it was to
stick a knife in him
[*Slowly*] Cassius was looking for something.
He wanted to be forgiven . . .
He wanted me to forgive him . . .
He wanted Herod to forgive him . . .
[*A laugh from the audience*]
Laugh if you like but I didn't think it funny
Because you see I could think of people who *would* forgive him,
On certain conditions,
And it was for someone like this that Cassius was looking.
What appealed to Cassius about Herod was that Herod was a
Jew.

[*A pause*]
He had found the wrong Jew.
But someday someone like Cassius would find the *right* Jew
And then there would be trouble.
[*A pause*]
What I learned from Cassius
Through those long boring evenings before Philippi
Was at least in the end interesting :
There was something in the Gentiles that needed the Jews . . .
A shiver ran down my spine
Because I could now foresee
The coming of Christianity . . .
[*The stage goes entirely dark*]

HEROD'S VOICE [*from the darkness, low*] : God of the Jews
Portable God
Immovable God
Inquisitive God
Historical God
God running for Mayor
God like a low fever
God trundled around
In an empty box
Empty box, empty tomb
The higher law
Of permanent uproar
The city destroyed

And the people scattered
Spores of infection
Bits of Jews
All over the place
Bits of God
    [*A pause*]
[*With rising emotion*] My city overthrown
My rational humorous city
City of an understood and accepted order
Conservative City comfortable City
City of a certain amount of fun
City of Man's acceptance
Of how he actually is
City of Greeks as well as Jews and of a certain jaunty
                                               impartiality
City not of the native Jews – the poisonous thistles of Sinai –
But of my friends the Jews from the Diaspora
Cosmopolitan people
Cultivated music-lovers
Whose children are now in New York
City with a Hippodrome as well as a Temple
City unpretentious except in the lavish jollity of externals
Real city destroyed by the desert winds of unreality
By the folly of men and
The arrogant unmannerly impossible
God of the Jews.
    [*A pause*]
What have they done to thee, city of Herod?
What have they done to thee
O my Jerusalem?
    [*Light on* HEROD, *his face in his hands*]

A VOICE: As a Jew I protest against this blasphemy against the
                                             Jewish faith!

SECOND VOICE: The Jew is blaspheming!

A VOICE: Herod!
    [*Herod raises his head. Silence*]

VOICE: Is that why you murdered the children?
    [*A pause*]

HEROD [*quietly*]: What about it?
  The children I really killed were my own.
  No business of yours.
  And it was to save the city that I killed them,
  My city.
    [*A pause*]
  I tried to save the city –
  The real city.
  That is what Herod is for.
  Don't expect me to go on about it like Cassius.
  The children are dead – that's all.
  They would be dead now anyway.
  And there are enough children as it is, aren't there?
    [*Rising, speaking with animation*]
  In any case you Papists have no right to complain!
  If you won't have contraception how can you control the
                                                  population

  Without the assistance of Herod?
  You ought to be grateful –

VOICES: Insulting the Church!
  Talking smut!
  Leave religion out of this!
    [HEROD *raises his hand*]

HEROD: All right, I don't expect to convince you. I don't blame you.
  You are prejudiced against me
  From what you heard about me
  In your own childhood, a time when
  You had a sincere aversion to people
  Who went around murdering children.
    [*A pause*]
  You would think that as parents
  You might be capable of forming a more broadminded view.
  But let me get on with my story,
  With, I hope, not quite so many interruptions.
  My leader Cassius was defeated,
  To my infinite relief,
  At the great battle of Philippi.

When he fell upon his sword
I ceased to be a Republican.
I took the oath
To Mark Anthony, Emperor of the East.
Yes, yes, the same Anthony –
Anthony and Cleopatra,
Or rather Cleopatra and Anthony.
My life you know alternates between the Bible
And the Roman history of Plutarch and Shakespeare.
Herod you see is at the foundation of your whole culture –
Such as it is:
Roman, Judaean, Christian –
The lot!
   [*A pause*]
With Anthony at least things were no longer boring.
Anthony liked me,
He had a sense of humour,
A robust sense of humour,
As befits a political man,
And it was he who made me King of the Jews.
That is what I mean by diplomacy:
Having been on the losing side to be able to get promotion
From the victorious enemy.
The trouble with Anthony was not conscience –
It was if anything worse –
It was women.
Anthony's Cleopatra and my Mariamne.
   [*A pause*]
You I expect when you hear the word Cleopatra
Think about Elizabeth Taylor.
If thinking it can be called.
Well, Cleopatra wasn't quite like that.
She was a bossy little bitch with a big bottom,
Little beady eyes,
A vindictive disposition,
And a flow of conversation
Of infinite lack of variety.
The only true thing Shakespeare said about her
Was that she was a serpent.

She was that all right.
As a matter of fact she tried to wrap herself round me
In the cold winter of 40 BC
At Alexandria when Anthony was in Rome,
I was a remarkably handsome young man in those days
If you like the Arab style of beauty, as Cleopatra did.
I looked like a Hollywood sheik, but more romantic in
                                                    appearance
Than in temperament.
I didn't find Cleopatra especially attractive,
I had in any case ten wives of my own
And there was also Anthony to be thought about and the
                                    politics of the thing
Which were remarkably bad politics.
So I shook myself loose and went on to Rome to meet Anthony.
The serpent never forgave me. She tried to bite.
   [*A pause*]
This Cleopatra was also the very good friend
Of another prominent serpent:
My mother-in-law
The notorious,
The pernicious
The really rather tiresome
Alexandra the Hasmonean.
And Alexandra meant also Mariamne,
My wife, and Aristobulus and Alexander,
My sons, to whom I have already referred.
My situation was one of peril.
Not only did the serpent of the Nile
Wind herself muddily into my family –
Which was bad enough –
But she thereby insinuated her odious person
Into the religious politics of Palestine . . .
   [*Spotlight off* HEROD *and on to the lay-figure*]
Here once again
In an unexpected form
Was that ominous convergence
Of the religion of the Jews
And the politics of the Gentiles.

I alone, the politic, impenetrable, insulating King of the Jews,
Standing like Aaron between the living and the dead,
Could still avert that confrontation –
But only by resolute, unsentimental action.
    [*Light on* HEROD *once more*]
You see I had married above my station.
From a Jewish point of view –
And this after all was the point of view of my subjects –
I was an Edomite or, if you prefer, an Idumean;
That is to say, a sort of Jewish Arab
And the Jews even in those days held Arabs in low esteem
And that included Jewish Arabs.
My wife on the other hand belonged to a *Hasmonean* family,
Very grand according to Jewish ideas, royal indeed,
And also priestly which was the same thing.
Priests were the Jewish idea of high society,
I don't know if you can understand that.
Politically it had been an excellent match
At first.
You see it was precisely because I was an Edomite and not a
                                            real Jew
That the Romans knew they could trust me.
I would support Rome because I needed Roman support.
They also knew that I knew this.
And they knew I was a man who acted on the basis of what he
                                            knew
And not on the basis of an inspiration from Jehovah.
Thus the fact of being a despised Edomite
Was a positive factor in my external relations.
But for domestic purposes, in my own kingdom,
To assure my authority, I needed to be more respectable –
                                    and this I became
Through marrying into a Hasmonean family . . .
So that everything was beautiful in my political garden
Before the serpent.
    [*A pause. Light back on the figure*]
Once Cleopatra encouraged
Alexandra, all the madness
Of the Jews began to break loose.

They thought themselves within reach of a Hasmonean
                                               kingdom,
A theocracy
The City of God
A truly Jewish state under the supreme lordship of none other
                                               than Jehovah
The end of Roman tutelage
The end of the sordid politics of the possible
The end of the scheming, Hellenized Edomite
The victory of the Law!
If I had let them go on they would have smashed the state
As they did smash it later on when my strong hand was
                                               withdrawn.
   [*Light back on* HEROD *who rises*]
So I took a deep breath, and the greatest and wisest risk in my
                                               career:
I decided to brave the wrath of Cleopatra
By murdering my mother-in-law.
Murder is sometimes politic but there are also times I must
                                               confess
When murder is a positive pleasure.
It wouldn't have been good policy to murder her all at once,
                                               of course.
The thing was to try out the ground, to get Anthony's reaction.
This I did by drowning my brother-in-law –
   [*Murmurs in the audience*]
Cleopatra was furious, but Anthony took the thing in good
                                               part,
As one of those rough, domestic pleasantries which fit the part
Of the oriental potentate, the picturesque vassal.
I had got away with it and could now afford to despatch, as I did,
All my Jewish relations.

VOICES : Get off the stage you dirty monster!
   Even if they were Jews that was still a mortal sin!

HEROD : You didn't say,
   'Get off the stage you dirty monster!'
   To President Kennedy at the time of the Bay of Pigs,
   Or even to President Truman at the time of Hiroshima,

Or to President Johnson . . .

VOICES: Leave Kennedy out of this!
That was war!
Kennedy didn't kill his own family!

HEROD: The people whom a statesman must kill
In war or in peace
Are those whom it is politically relevant to kill.
In my day the people who were politically relevant
Were dynastic people, members of the family
Of the successful statesman.
I loved Mariamne, Aristobulus and Alexander,
And had I lived in a political context such as your own
I would not have found it either relevant or rewarding
To put them to death.
As it is my hands are guiltless
Of the blood
Of any Cubans, Koreans, Japanese or Vietnamese,
Or for that matter of members of the Irish Republican Army,
It is all a question of context.
President Kennedy being a successful statesman
Was necessarily a person very much like myself
    [*Murmurs of disapproval from the audience*]
Ruthless and realistic.
He shed the blood that had to be shed in his own particular
                                                    situation
For the preservation of the state
And of his own power.
For him that meant a certain number of Cubans, Vietnamese,
                                                    etc.

But had President Kennedy found himself in *my* situation,
Why then, he would have had to kill the persons whose deaths
    were inscribed in the logic of that particular situation, and
                                                    no other,
And that would have meant that President Kennedy,
A gentleman for whom I have
The greatest respect,
Would not have hesitated to order the murder
Of Jackie,

Of Caroline
And of little John–John.

[*Uproar in the theatre.* HEROD *seems disconcerted by the volume
of disapproval; for the first time he shows traces of agitation*]

HEROD : Please, ladies and gentlemen,
I didn't mean to insult President Kennedy.
I was trying to explain
Myself.
I ask you to have the courtesy to give a hearing
To an old gentleman who has had, after all,
A fairly distinguished career.
My story is nearing its end.
Where was I?
Oh yes, we were approaching
The great Battle of Actium,
The sea-fight that Anthony lost, you remember?
I would have been at the great Battle of Actium
On the losing side, had it not been for Cleopatra
Whose idea was of course to keep me
From my share of the *victory*.
So after the death of the serpent – at which I rejoiced –
I was forced to make my peace with the victorious Caesar
                                                    Augustus

Who recognized me as king,
   increased my dominions,
   and had the curious idea
   of presenting me
With Cleopatra's Celtic bodyguard.
I think it must have been his idea of a joke
To present a prominent Jewish politician
With a bunch of Irish cops.
So now I was firmly established
Through my extraordinary political sagacity,
On the side of the ultimate victor of all the wars,
At the right hand of Caesar Augustus.
Augustus, like the Governments of Russia and the United
                                                    States today,
Believed in allowing small countries to have nominal
                                                    sovereignty,

Provided their rulers in practice obeyed him
In matters about which he was concerned.
This was known as indirect rule, and it was a system that I
                                    thoroughly understood.
Augustus was the indirect ruler, but I in my smaller way was
                                    also an indirect ruler –
One of the most indirect rulers of all time.
We understood one another.
    [*Sitting down, with an air of weariness and bitterness*]
The same unfortunately could not be said of my subjects,
The bloody Jews.
They hated indirect rule,
They said it was a sham
And shams were something up with which the Lord God of
                                    Israel
Could not put.
It was a sham all right,
A sham with which you could live.
After my death they got what they were looking for:
The bracing shock of reality –
Direct Roman rule.
Pontius Pilate Governor of Judaea
And then Titus and the destruction of the Temple!
They can't say I didn't do my best for them –
I even tried to solve the religious problem
By my own application of indirect rule.
I used to keep the High Priest's robes in my house
    [*Gestures towards the lay-figure*]
And hire them out to whoever I would hire as High Priest.
    [*Rises, speaking like an auctioneer*]
Ladies and gentlemen, I have an announcement to make.
A vacancy has arisen and a senior appointment has to be made.
The post is permanent and pensionable.
The salary scale begins at £10000 per annum and rises by
                                    annual increments of £1000
To £15000.
There is also a Representation allowance of £5000 per annum
Which is free of tax.
No particular qualifications are required

Except the ability to keep a straight face in public
And absolute willingness to carry out without question
Whatever instructions may be issued from time to time
By Herod . . .
 [*A pause*]
May I ask any persons who wish to apply for this post
To stand up?
 [*A number of members of the audience hurriedly rise to their
 feet. Other persons enter and form a queue in the aisle*]

HEROD [*surveying the scene*]: I am glad to see that some of you
at least

Are prepared to reconsider your views of Herod
In a flexible and broadminded way
Given suitable incentives . . .
Oh, there was one point I forgot:
The applicant must be a Jew.

ANGRY VOICES: Discrimination! No Irish need apply!
 Boycott Herod!
 This is worse than Derry!
 [*One member of the audience steps up on the stage*]

HEROD: Gentlemen, gentlemen, you are being unreasonable.
 The post which is vacant is that of High Priest of Jerusalem.
 I know you Dubliners have had a Jewish Lord Mayor –
 But when have you had a Jewish Archbishop of Dublin?
 [*A pause*]
 Very well then.
 [*To the man who has stepped on the stage*] What is your name?

MAN: My name is Annas, your Majesty.

HEROD: No. I know you, your name is Caiaphas.

MAN: My name is Caiaphas, your Majesty.

HEROD: Don't contradict me, you impudent blackguard –
 You told me yourself your name was Annas.

MAN: I am extremely sorry, your Majesty. Annas, at your
Majesty's service.

HEROD : All right, High Priest, you've made your point –
Come here.

> [HEROD *hurriedly and as if with distaste invests* ANNAS/
> CAIAPHAS *with the High Priest's robes. He makes a poor job of it.*
> HEROD *stands back and looks at his High Priest*]

HEROD : Christ! You look a proper Charlie!
The Pharisees will eat you.
Oh well, we can always get another –
There are plenty more where *you* come from.
Well, what are you waiting for?
Don't just stand there.
Go away and offer sacrifice or something –
Keep the show on the road!

> HEROD's *High Priest shambles off down the aisle amid the
> jeers of the audience.* HEROD *resumes his seat, knocking
> over the dummy as he does so*]

HEROD : As you can see, my religious policy
Was not an unqualified success.
But then if it had been an unqualified success it would have
                              been a failure, if you see what I mean.
What I really had to have was Rome's approval and that was
                                        only available
To a King of the Jews who was known to be execrated by his
                              pious subjects.
So the cries of execration
And the smell of burning Pharisee
Were an important part of the story of my success.
They went down well in Rome.
> [*A pause*]
The Pharisees, you know, were not at all like your idea of them.
You, from your vague and intermittent contacts with the
                              Gospels,
Think of them as stuffy bourgeois, who were snooty to barmen,
And were self-righteous about peculiarities of that order.
That wasn't it at all.
The Pharisees were more like the New Left –
Prickly people,

Dandies about their consciences,
Brave, stupid and disputatious,
Daring one another along the road to martyrdom.
Confrontation was what they liked
And they got it.
They needed me.
And I needed them.
They tore down the Eagle from the Temple,
Assaulting the symbol of secular sovereignty,
Asserting the supremacy of their Higher Law.
So, of course, I burned these Pharisees in considerable numbers
To the accompaniment of appropriate publicity.
   [*A pause*]
Thus I gave satisfaction to Caesar Augustus
And it must be supposed that the Pharisees gave satisfaction –
To what? To whom?
   [*A pause*]
Never mind. It was in the sombre glare of these events –
Which served my modest human purpose and as they thought
                           reflected the Divine Will –
That my long successful and indeed brilliant reign drew to its
                                       close.

I died a great King,
Respected throughout the Empire which was then at the zenith
Of the last years before Christ.
It is true that for a time
In Judaea itself
Men rejoiced at my death.
But they did not rejoice for long . . .
The imbecility of my successors
And the enormous disasters
They brought upon Israel
Soon convinced even the Jews
Of the profound wisdom of my proceedings.
Among the Pharisees themselves the wisest men
Worked for a Herodian restoration.
All looked back with pride
To the life and times of good King Herod.
   [*A pause. The sound of a baby crying is heard.*

HEROD *sits absolutely still, rigidly upright. The crying ceases.*
HEROD *remains motionless. A pause*]

SINGER'S VOICE: And Kings sat still with awful eye
As if they surely knew their Sovereign Lord was by.

HEROD [*in a low, controlled but tense voice*]:
I do not know whether this is an intrigue of Cleopatra,
Of perhaps a provocation of the Pharisees,
Or whether it may not be quite simply that some member
of the audience
Unable to find a sitter
Has brought a baby to the theatre –

SINGER'S VOICE: He feels from Judah's land
The dreaded Infant's hand.

HEROD: Whatever it is, it must not occur again!
[*His voice trembles slightly*] You must take the child home!
This is no place for a baby!
Can you not see for yourself
That it is wrong?
It's worse than that! It's cruel!
[*His voice breaks*] That's what it is: cruel!
[*He sobs for a moment or two, and then regains
control, but in a more intimate manner different from his
earlier one*]

HEROD [*sadly*]: That's what it is all right,
That's what I left out.
No one is as politic, no one as calculating
As I made myself out to be.
You can be as politic as you wish during the day but when you
wake in the middle of the night
As I increasingly did –
Wakened by a child crying
A child who wasn't there
My own or another –
There is no politics at three in the morning.
I was a man possessed by the ordinary human passions
Which include cruelty, and my position placed me –

As yours does not – in a position to gratify them all,
As they say, but gratification
Is hardly an appropriate way of expressing what really happens.
I killed Mariamne, not really because of the political and
                                            religious
Conjuncture in Palestine,
But because I loved her, and was jealous, and could not sleep,
                                            and had the power
To do what I thought I wanted to do;
I was ashamed to tell you the full story about that
Because it is such a sordid episode.
You see my mother-in-law, the Hasmonean monster,
Alexandra,
Seeking to improve her political prospects
Had the bright idea of sending to Anthony,
Emperor of the East,
The portraits of two very beautiful young people –
Her daughter Mariamne, my wife,
And her son Aristobulus, my brother-in-law.
Her calculations were rather obvious.
Anthony's tastes were, as they say,
Catholic, though not in the sense in which that term
Is generally used among you.
Now this same Anthony as well as being broadminded
And inquisitive in sexual matters –
Which is why he was out of training when he had to fight the
                                            great Battle of Actium –
Also prided himself on being a gentleman
And was in fact a moderately competent second-class politician.
So despite the enticements of our family pimp
He refrained from sending for my wife Mariamne.
And it immediately became heart-breakingly obvious
That my wife Mariamne
Was bitterly disappointed at not being invited
And was frantically jealous of her brother's good fortune.
For her brother Aristobulus was in fact summoned
By the Emperor himself to the imperial brothel
In Alexandria.
By this time poor Herod was almost mad

With jealousy about Mariamne, hatred of Alexandra, and the
                                 most lively political fear
Aroused by the thought of that wretched Aristobulus
Advancing the politics of Alexandra in the bed of Anthony
And sodomizing his way to the downfall and death of Herod . . .
For a political man the only solace
Is energetic politics so I applied my political energy
To Aristobulus, the most pressing of my problems.
When he was bathing one morning his lively young playmates
Boisterously ducked him and when they had done ducking him
He was dead.
When I reported to Anthony that unfortunately his package
Had been spoiled by water
He laughed it off: possibly he was afraid of Cleopatra.
After that, moving with more assurance,
I stepped on that scorpion, the pious Hasmonean,
My wife's mother.
The only trouble with that was that my wife
Holding me in horror took to herself a lover
Called I believe Joseph or some such name.
I struck out blindly
Not as a politician but as a wounded man
I killed them both and then it had to be the turn of my sons
                                 by Mariamne
For the most basic of all political reasons:
It was them or me.
    [*A pause*]
By the time we were through with the repercussions
Of Alexandra's dirty picture postcards
There was nothing at all left of my wife's family –
And of Herod himself
Nothing but a grim, impressive and still formidable hulk.
    [*A pause*]
It would be hard to find a purely political explanation
For my attempt to kill myself.
Yes, towards the end I tried suicide
Like poor old Cassius, but unlike him
I made a botch of it . . . with a fruit-knife . . .
    [*A pause*]

Poor Cassius!
   [*A pause*]
You can see now what I am trying to say?
Why I have had to talk to you in this manner
At such inordinate length and so deviously?
I am asking you in the name of the little Herods shut up in
                                        your own bosoms
Only awaiting a suitable opportunity of self-expression;
I am asking you in the name of the permanent need which
                              you have as political animals
For some kind of Herod –
A master politician – a man who gets things done;
Things, and people;
I am asking you in the name of a terrible thing –
Our common humanity –
I am asking you because in all of you there is something
      which would like to do what I have done, and be what I
                                        have been.

   [*He falls on his knees*]
I am asking you to give me that which I contemptuously
                              withheld from Cassius

In his boring agony before Philippi
I am asking your forgiveness,
Forgiveness for Herod the Great,
The King of the Jews.

CURTAIN

Salome and the Wild Man
or
The Quiet Galilean

Cast

PHILO, a Sophist

SALOME, a Princess

THE WILD MAN

POSTUMUS, a Roman security officer

This play has not been performed. It was given a public reading by students of the University of Kent, at Canterbury, in 1972.

Salome and the Wild Man

Scene

The school of PHILO *the Sophist at Alexandria, indicated by a placard bearing that legend; the stage otherwise bare. As the curtain rises,* PHILO, SALOME *and the* WILD MAN *are walking round and round the stage.* PHILO *is a middle-aged Levantine, a stocky man tending to fat, but active and even bouncy; the* WILD MAN *is young, small, bony, dirty and restless:* SALOME *is young, dark and beautiful, and moves like a dancer, which she has to be. The* WILD MAN *is dressed in a sleeveless belted tunic made of rather mangy-looking skins.* PHILO *and* SALOME *are dressed in neat and simple versions of the Greek dress of approximately the second decade of the Christian era. The contrast between the upper-class appearance of* PHILO *and* SALOME *and the recalcitrant figure of the* WILD MAN *should be striking.*

PHILO [*professional tone*]: What is freedom? . . . Salome?

SALOME [*easily*]: Freedom, dear master, is being oneself.
[*The* WILD MAN *spits. They stop walking*]

PHILO [*still to* SALOME]: The wild man, being himself, spits.
Is freedom, then, spitting?

SALOME: Obviously it is, for the wild man. But not for me.

PHILO: Well, wild man, is spitting your only answer to the
question?

WILD MAN [*tone of a refractory student*]: In substance, yes. But
for the sake of practice I am prepared to elaborate. I hope
you understand what I am practising? To beat the Romans
we must understand their weapons, and we then use them
when they suit our needs. And one of their weapons is
sophistry. Their cheapest weapon. [*Looks at* PHILO *apprais-
ingly*] A fellow like you, for example, I should say . . .
[*Rubs the philosopher's mantle between finger and thumb*]

PHILO [*calmly, withdrawing his mantle*]: I am not a Roman,
I am a Greek.

SALOME [*laughing*]: A Greek called Philo the Jew!

PHILO [*with dignity*]: Exactly. A Greek called Philo the Jew.
Civilization: Greek. Religion: Jewish. [*The* WILD MAN
begins to growl and moves towards PHILO] Object in life: to
attain a harmony between Greek and Jew within the Roman
empire. [*The* WILD MAN *flings himself on* PHILO *who holds
him off easily and continues, while* SALOME *laughs*] A harmony,
my dear wild man, a *harmony*, which will be the beauty and

the majesty of all future culture on this planet. A small
matter in your eyes, my urgent wild man. . . . But in the
meantime you are wasting your own time, your urgent time,
not mine. You want to learn the weapons of the Romans?
Their basic weapon is self-control, the art of striking only
at the appropriate moment. [*The* WILD MAN *relaxes his
grip and* PHILO *steps back.* PHILO *continues*] Another fine
weapon is courtesy, something like a net. . . . But that is
in the advanced course: I doubt if you will get that far. . . .
You have learned at any rate this much: if you are paying
a fencing-master it is foolish to go for him with a club.

SALOME [*mildly interested*]: Paying? I thought I was your only
paying pupil. I thought you took the wild man for the
fun of the thing . . .

WILD MAN [*still panting a little*]: I pay him nothing.

PHILO: You pay me all right. You are studying me in order
to fight me. Is that right, wild man?

WILD MAN [*recovering himself*]: Dead right, sophist Philo, Jew
Philo, Greek Philo, Roman Philo. I will fight you till I
have killed all of you.

PHILO [*earnestly*]: I believe you, wild man, and that is why I
admitted you to my school, and tolerate your atrocious
manners and dismal appearance, [*sniffing*] and other
characteristics. You are studying me, because I am your
enemy – which is absolutely true – but I am also studying
you, because you are *my* enemy, the deadly and permanent
enemy of civilization.

WILD MAN: Not of civilization: of injustice and oppression.

PHILO: They are all the same thing, wild man. Your dirt and
your skins and your stink know it, if you don't. If you
don't understand your own message how can you understand
mine? . . . You are studying me, then, and I am studying
you. Which will learn faster, do you think, Salome?

SALOME [*sweetly*]: I think, dear master, that you are making
a lot of mistakes this morning, and that the one you have

just made is particularly bad. What I am *supposed* to say is too clearly indicated. If I were a poor student of course – in any sense of the word – I should follow your lead and say that you, the great Philo, the profound Philo, will study harder and learn faster than the poor savage, who will always be outwitted. But I don't *have* to say that. I am brilliant, beautiful, rich and of royal blood. I should imagine that the remittances you receive from my stepfather the Tetrarch are about your only source of revenue. So I shall say what I like.

PHILO [*smiling*]: What an agreeable class I have this morning: a smelly savage and a rich bitch!

WILD MAN: Careful, Philo, remember where the money comes from!

SALOME: If he were careful he wouldn't amuse me, and he knows it. . . . You know, I suppose, wild man, that that is really why *you* are here: not for him to study you, but for you to amuse me? That is what sophists and wild men are for: the entertainment of the rich and beautiful.

WILD MAN: I shall entertain you, Salome, one day.

SALOME: How, wild man? Will you dance for me, wild man? [*A pause*]
Please dance for me, wild man, a wild wild dance? [*She holds out her arms to him: he remains impassive. She herself begins to dance.* PHILO *at first watches with amusement.* SALOME, *finding her long robe in the way of her dancing, begins to take if off*]

PHILO [*alarmed*]: Salome, please, remember the servants! A lot of them are Africans! Your stepfather won't like this at all! This might cause very serious trouble! [SALOME, *smiling, watches first* PHILO *then the* WILD MAN]

WILD MAN [*beginning to chuckle*]: You're right, Philo, so it might! Trouble! All right, Salome, let's dance! [*The* WILD MAN *tears off his skin coat.* SALOME *sheds her robe: this is done simply – no 'seven veils' nonsense. Cheers from off-stage.* PHILO *holds his head in his hands*]

SALOME [*shouting off-stage*]: Boys! Drums!

PHILO [*groaning*]: And these are *students*! This is a *school*!
Oh Socrates!
[*Exit* PHILO *as the drums begin.* SALOME *and the* WILD
MAN *dance a kind of African dance, with the distinct types
of frenzy appropriate to their personalities. When the dancing
stops, the* WILD MAN *holds* SALOME's *hands*]

WILD MAN [*gently and eagerly*]: Salome!

SALOME [*not quite conscious of her surroundings*]: What is it . . .
wild man?

WILD MAN: If you would join our movement . . .

SALOME [*smiling, withdraws her hands*]: Why not, I'm interested
in movement: all kinds of movement. . . . [*Begins to dress*]
But we must get our clothes on before the police come.

WILD MAN [*puzzled*]: Police?

SALOME [*finishing dressing*]: The Sophist has gone to fetch the
police. Sophists are always on the side of the police. You
have explained it to me yourself.

WILD MAN [*putting on his skins*]: If the Roman police come,
I must leave.

SALOME: What, and run around the city of Alexandria in
the peculiar uniform of a Jewish prophet? And that
expression? After Philo has given the alarm? You'd be cut
down by some centurion before the day was out – if the
Greek mob didn't get you first. Your only hope is to stay
where you are. Leave the rest to me.

WILD MAN [*with a kind of wary eagerness*]: Then you *are* on
my side, Salome?

SALOME [*carefully*]: I am on your side, wild man . . .
sufficiently to meet the needs of your present situation. . . .
Let me see. Because Philo is a Greek the Romans will keep
him waiting for about ten minutes . . . because he is a Jew
they will keep him waiting another ten minutes. But then
again if someone spots him as connected with the family

of an important Roman vassal princeling they would see him at once. Since the nearest military post is just down the road, the time available is somewhere between zero and twenty minutes . . . so tell me something about your life, or your movement or whatever you call it.

WILD MAN [*resolutely*]: When the Romans come I shall not lie to them. I shall . . .

SALOME: You will shut up completely, if you want to stay in business as a revolutionary. I shall say that all pious Jews are commanded to observe total silence between sunrise and sundown on the feast of the holy prophet Pentateuch. Romans will swallow anything in that line. But time is running out. If you want me to join your movement you must tell me what it is about . . .

WILD MAN: You *must* join us, Salome. We need you. The granddaughter of Herod the Great – who was King of the Jews after all, whatever his crimes – the descendant of the Maccabees, the highest blood of Israel, royal and priestly.

SALOME [*surprised*]: King? Highest? Royal? Priestly? What kind of a revolution is this, wild man?

WILD MAN: A Jewish revolution.

SALOME: Is that all?

WILD MAN: No, but it begins with the Jews . . . Listen, Salome:
There are only two peoples in the world: the Romans and the Jews.
There are only two Gods in the world: Caesar and Jehovah . . .
Caesar is what man is. Jehovah is what he must be.
The world is covered by the tissue of the politics of Caesar –
Not only by his material power, his triremes and his legions . . .
[SALOME *begins to dance a slow and stately dance, hieratic and faintly cruel, with a touch of dignified corruption. The* WILD MAN *continues as if seeing a vision*]

Not only by the administrative filaments of his governors,
procurators and vassal-kings
Not only by taxes collected by mercenaries and returning
always in the form of more mercenaries
Not only by the always open choice between slavery
and crucifixion,
Not only by spies and the simpler forms of bribery,
But by the massive corruption of intelligence and through
intelligence of all mankind
The abasement of the Greek mind into the service of the
imperial idea
The creation of intellectual prisons side by side with the
material ones in every province
The academy beside the police station
Philo the Sophist hand in hand with Herod the Tetrarch
The creation of an architecture of ideas
Intricate, ceremonious and authoritative
Confined to the sole perspective of the possible
The politics of the possible being an alley which always
debouches into a square
Of which the centre is an equestrian statue of Caesar
Surrounded by slaves, traitors and corpses . . .
[*A pause*]
Yet there is another politics: the politics of the
impossible . . .
[*The rhythm of* SALOME's *dance changes. It becomes grave
and austere with a suggestion of restrained wrath and menace*]
Of this politics the Jews are the carriers
Whether they like it or not wherever they carry their
Book
They carry the idea of the higher law
The idea which negates Caesar
The idea which gnaws the whole vast structure of the
Empire
And must one day bring it crashing down
Setting free the slaves
Cleansing the corrupted mind
Shattering the idols
Setting free the creative powers of man

In a society of justice, equality and love.
[SALOME *stops dancing*]

SALOME: I can believe the bit about the Book, the gnawing
and the crashing: I think it's beginning to happen. But the
'society of justice' and all the rest of it – I wonder whether
you can really believe it yourself? After all the Jews, who
already *have* the Book and the higher law don't behave
all that well, do they?

WILD MAN [*with animation*]: That's just it, Salome! That's the
point of our movement. We don't want corrupt Jews, or
Jews only. We are a revolutionary society, open to all –
Jews and non-Jews – who will pledge themselves solemnly
to self-abnegation in the service of the higher law, to
absolute rejection of the blasphemous claims of Caesar,
and to armed struggle for the overthrow of Roman power.
We have a cleansing ceremony which I ask you to undergo.
It is called . . .

SALOME [*change of tone*]: Shut up, wild man, and stay quiet
whatever I say. Here they are.
[*Enter* PHILO *and* POSTUMUS. POSTUMUS *is a burly
elderly man with the look of a policeman nearing retirement.*
PHILO *shows signs of agitation*]

PHILO: This is Princess Salome of Galilee . . . and that is the
young scoundrel I told you about.

POSTUMUS [*bowing to* SALOME *with slightly perfunctory
deference*]: Good morning, your Highness. I am sorry to
disturb you. [*To* WILD MAN] Come along with me, you
scum. [*The* WILD MAN *does not move or speak but stands
very erect looking* POSTUMUS *in the eye.* POSTUMUS *moves
forward as if to strike him*]

SALOME [*in a loud clear voice with a commanding tone*]: One
moment, Captain. [POSTUMUS *looks round, startled*] You are
in the Tenth Legion, are you not?

POSTUMUS: Yes, your Highness.

SALOME: Service in Palestine?

POSTUMUS [*a little impatiently, looking towards the* WILD MAN]:
Yes . . .

SALOME: You are perhaps old enough to have served with
my grandfather, King Herod the Great?

POSTUMUS [*showing interest*]: Yes, your Highness. In the
Parthian war. Your grandfather was a fine soldier and a
great man for a . . .

SALOME [*softly*]: For a Jew . . . [POSTUMUS *looks startled.*
PHILO *looks in alarm from* POSTUMUS *to* SALOME] What is
your name, Captain?

POSTUMUS: Postumus, your Highness.

SALOME: I think you have forgotten something, Postumus.
It is true that my grandfather was King of the Jews. He was
also adopted by the late Emperor, the Divine Augustus . . .
[POSTUMUS *stands to attention*] into the Imperial House,
the Julian clan itself. Thus, in the opinion of the Divine
Augustus, our family are not merely Romans, but among
the very noblest Romans, attached to the family of the God
Caesar. [*The* WILD MAN *flinches.* PHILO *looks increasingly
alarmed.* POSTUMUS *stands rigidly*] Are you of the same
opinion as the Divine Augustus, and his divine successors . . .
Captain Postumus?

POSTUMUS [*bowing deeply and speaking inarticulately*]: Your
Royal Highness! I am sorry. . . .

SALOME: It is possible indeed that you may be sorry, Captain
Postumus. We shall see. In the meantime you understand
that, before taking any further action on whatever report
has been made to you by my stepfather's employee, you
will report to me?

POSTUMUS: Yes, your Royal Highness.

PHILO: As the Princess's tutor . . .

SALOME [*to* PHILO]: It remains to be seen whether you are
still the Princess's tutor. [*To* POSTUMUS, *more graciously*]
Well, then, please tell me what this is all about?

POSTUMUS: Philo here, your Highness, reported that this fellow [*nodding at the* WILD MAN] engaged – tried to engage – your Highness in some kind of indecent dance. He said it might have a ritual significance. He said it might constitute an effort to draw your Highness into revolutionary activity.

SALOME [*laughing*]: Really, Captain Postumus! Do I look as if I was in the habit of engaging in indecent ritual– revolutionary dances with dirty little students dressed in rabbit skins?

POSTUMUS: No indeed, your Highness. But you see I had to check on the report because this man is already under suspicion, in connection with disturbances on the Judaea– Galilee border. At the time he left there, there were some serious outbreaks of baptism . . .

PHILO: Outbreaks of *what?*

POSTUMUS: Baptism. It is the oath-taking ceremony of a revolutionary society. Anti-Roman. All sorts of filthy practices connected with it. Has to be stamped out. [*Looking longingly at the* WILD MAN *who stares back*]

SALOME: Indeed yes, Captain. Of course it must be stamped out. My family has more to lose by that sort of thing than you have. . . . But you know, Postumus, one must proceed with great caution in these Jewish matters. Sometimes, you see, the *real* anti-Roman accuses the *pro*-Roman of being *anti*-Roman in order to get him into trouble. [POSTUMUS *scratches his head*] It is easy to burn one's fingers. . . . You want to know what really happened here today?

POSTUMUS: Yes, your Highness.

SALOME: This is a delicate political matter, Captain. I should like to discuss it with you personally.

POSTUMUS [*deferentially*]: Of course, your Royal Highness. [*To the* WILD MAN *in a brutal tone*] All right, you get out of here till I call you. Don't try to leave the building. We have men at all exits with orders to kill anyone trying to escape. [*Exit* WILD MAN]

SALOME: This was simply a quarrel between two Jews, both of them rather silly and harmless. Philo, who fancies himself as a sort of honorary Greek, was going on about the superiority of Greek culture over both Jewish and Roman. Rabbit-skin, who is a pious Jew, tried to hit him, so Philo tried to get him run in. Simple . . .

PHILO: You can question the servants . . .

SALOME: How my grandfather would have laughed! Tell him why you won't question the servants, Postumus.

POSTUMUS: This is not a school, Philo. You don't question servants, administratively, until you know what you want them to say. Then you make them say it. We're not at that stage. But I could question the suspect . . .

SALOME: I think not, Postumus. By the way, do we really need Philo here for all this? [POSTUMUS *jerks his thumb. Exit* PHILO] First of all the wild man cannot, being a devout Jew, speak at all at present. You know, of course, from your Palestine days, that this is the eve of the great festival of Septuagint?

POSTUMUS: Oh, ah.

SALOME: So you see how matters stand . . .

POSTUMUS: Yes, your Highness. But we can question him anyway. If he doesn't talk today, he'll talk tomorrow . . .

SALOME [*in a detached tone*]: It was my grandfather's experience that many of these fanatical Jews will die under torture rather than talk.

POSTUMUS [*surer of his ground*]: I know, your Highness. There are always some casualties in the course of interrogation. We must expect this.

SALOME: Of course, Captain. But you must be sure that you get the right casualties. . . . It is your responsibility . . .

POSTUMUS [*hesitates*]: But your Highness, this fellow is obviously a fanatic . . .

SALOME [*laughs*] : I'm afraid Palestine didn't make much impression on you, Captain! Of course he's a fanatic. The whole country is crawling with fanatics. But there are fanatics and fanatics: dangerous ones and useful ones – useful to Rome that is. There are, in fact, *our* fanatics and *theirs*. This fellow is one of ours. Not that he's pro-Roman: he would be less useful to the Romans if he were. You see he preaches some kind of spiritual kingdom, non-violence and so on. In practice, submission to Roman rule. My stepfather doesn't know what he would do without people like that. Pontius Pilate, in Judaea, is of the same opinion, and the governor of Syria approves the policy. All this would receive a grave setback if word reached Palestine – and you know how the Jews talk – that the apostle of non-violence had been tortured to death by the Romans. His following would join the Zealots, the revolutionaries – sorry, Captain, what's this you call them officially?

POSTUMUS : *Latrones*, your Highness. Bandits. That's what they are.

SALOME : Of course, Captain. So you see the result? Trouble in Palestine. Displeasure in Rome at the cost of having to suppress it. Enquiry into what happened in Alexandria. Captain Postumus before a commission of enquiry . . . Caesar does not forgive errors that cost money to repair.

POSTUMUS [*looking creased, baffled and sweaty*]: Your Highness, I am a plain soldier. I hate politics. Especially . . . [*He pauses*]

SALOME [*smiling*]: *Jewish* politics? God knows I don't blame you.

POSTUMUS : Well, yes, your Highness. I'm out of my depth, quite frankly. It's clear you know what's what. . . . [*In a tone of one expecting advice*] I suppose the safest thing for me to do is to take no action now, and submit the question for the decision of my superiors.

SALOME [*nodding*]: That might be the right thing, Captain. [*A pause*] . . . I don't know about it's being the *safest*

thing. [*Dreamily*] Let me see . . . The report goes to Rome,
of course. . . . Then the enquiries begin. Rome to Syria,
Governor of Syria to Procurator of Judaea . . . [*She moves
with her feet as if sketching a dance step*] Procurator to Tetrarch
. . . [*She smiles*] My stepfather takes to his bed. My mother
Herodias makes her counter-moves. She will see this as a
plot against *her* through an attempt to compromise her
daughter. The whole great family of Herod, and all the
Hasmoneans as well, will be persuaded they are in danger.
Uproar among influential Jews, first in Palestine and then
in Rome. What will Caesar do? . . . I don't know. The
easiest thing, and the *cheapest* thing, would be to decide that
a mistake had been made, an expensive mistake. Made
initially, as enquiry would show, by *you*, Captain Postumus.

POSTUMUS [*a noise between a grunt and a groan*]: Your
Highness . . . How can I get out of this?

SALOME: Get Philo to drop his charge.

POSTUMUS [*in a parade-ground roar*]: Philo!
[*Re-enter* PHILO, *looking flustered*]

POSTUMUS [*still roaring*]: You lying swine! [*He knocks* PHILO
down and starts to stamp on him]

SALOME [*in a tone of one dealing with a breach of etiquette*]:
Captain! Please remember where you are!
[POSTUMUS *steps back.* PHILO *picks himself up, badly
shaken*]

SALOME [*gently to* PHILO]: I'm sorry about this, Philo. If you
bring the police into an academy you never know where
it will end . . . If we're all to get any peace you'd better
admit you made up the whole story when you were in a
fit of temper with the wild man.

PHILO [*sulkily*]: I told the truth.

SALOME: The *truth*, Sophist? Try to be a little more
sophisticated. Stick to your story if you like. Go back to the
post with the Captain for a few days of soldierly
questioning . . . [PHILO *shudders*] Then await *in custody*

the outcome of an enquiry which in its later stages will
probably include your being broken on the wheel. . . . That's
one way of doing it. . . . Or else confess you made a mistake.
Then Captain Postumus will simply close his file and let
you go back to your work. Right, Captain?

POSTUMUS: *Right,* your Royal Highness.

PHILO [*slowly*]: I see. . . . Captain Postumus . . . I'm afraid
I made a mistake . . . I hope you will allow me to correct it?

POSTUMUS [*hugely relieved, guffaws*]: *That's* the boy. [*Slaps*
PHILO *on the back*] Come on back to the post, sign a statement withdrawing this cock-and-bull story of yours, and
we'll have a jug of wine together. [*To* SALOME] I am
deeply grateful to your Royal Highness . . . [SALOME *nods
graciously. Exeunt* POSTUMUS *and* PHILO]

SALOME [*raising her voice*]: Wild man! Come out, wild man!
[*Enter* WILD MAN]

WILD MAN [*suspiciously*]: What did you tell him?

SALOME [*smiling*]: I talked about you. I said you weren't really
as wild as you looked. I said you were one of the quiet
Galileans.

WILD MAN [*shouting*]: The *quiet* Galileans!

SALOME: Yes – *you* know – the ones who say you may
pay Caesar his taxes. The real revolution is of the spirit.
All that. Nice and safe. You know, wild man, I wish you
were like that. Then it would be safe to fall in love with you.

WILD MAN [*hurriedly and uncomfortably, in order to change the
subject*]: Did he believe you?

SALOME [*dreamily*]: Of course, if you *were* like that, I mightn't
want to fall in love with you. . . . What I want to fall in
love with may be the revolution – in you. Wouldn't that
be strange, wild man?

WILD MAN [*hoarsely and tormentedly*]: Salome, I haven't time
to talk about falling in love. The revolution is my whole
life. So I must know: *did he believe you?*

SALOME: I am Herod's granddaughter, wild man. I am a
very great lady. I am also very, very clever, my lovely,
brave, stupid, dirty wild man. So of course he believed
me. . . . He believed what I could do, not what I said. If
he hadn't believed me you would now be down at the
station, and they would be breaking the little bones in your
feet, as you should know, being a revolutionary. . . . Why
are the good people all so stupid, wild man?

WILD MAN: Cleverness is horrible, Salome.

SALOME: What do you know about it, wild man? Cleverness
is neither beautiful nor horrible: it is just necessary for
survival.

WILD MAN [*contemptuously*]: Survival of what? Survival *as*
what?

SALOME: Good questions, wild man. But not questions you
ask if you want to survive . . .

WILD MAN: I don't want to survive. Survival is for brutes.
I want to live and act, serving the revolution, and to die
when the service of the revolution requires it of me.

SALOME: I know all that, wild man, you look it, you smell
of it, you don't need to say it. The strange thing is that a
part of me would die if I could not follow you. But all of
me might die if I did. . . .

WILD MAN [*with timid hope*]: Salome!

SALOME [*gravely*]: Well, wild man?

WILD MAN: Salome, will you . . .

SALOME: Will I what, wild man?

WILD MAN [*resolutely*]: Will you allow me to baptize you?
[SALOME *bursts out laughing. The* WILD MAN *does not flinch.
From the moment he has asked this question he assumes a more
authoritative manner*]

SALOME: I'm sorry, wild man. It's just that the policeman
who was here said that baptism was frightfully indecent, so
that your proposal. . . .

WILD MAN [*firmly*]: You talk frivolously, Salome, because you were brought up among the corruptness of this vile Empire. Baptism means that you want to be clean, that you want to live with other human beings, in love and justice. . . .

SALOME: And peace?

WILD MAN: Justice comes before peace.

SALOME: That is the difference between you and the quiet Galileans?

WILD MAN: Yes, Salome. The quiet Galileans are traitors. They say you can have peace without justice. They are the servants of Caesar.

SALOME: So that the policeman was right about one thing: baptism means joining a revolutionary society?

WILD MAN: Exactly, Salome. That is what I am asking you to do. Will you do it?

SALOME: Wait a moment, wild man. I am accustomed to reasoning things out. . . .

WILD MAN: That is where the lies come in, Salome. Reasoning is lying to yourself. You know what you ought to do. Do it.

SALOME: I must go about this my own way, wild man. *Where* would you make your revolution?

WILD MAN: In the world. Throughout the Empire. But first of all in Palestine, because the Jews are ripe for revolution.

SALOME: In Palestine . . . including Galilee?

WILD MAN: It is to Galilee I must go first.

SALOME: To raise the people against my stepfather and my mother?

WILD MAN: Yes, Salome. They are so hated, and my following there is so great, that the Tetrarch and his so-called wife will be overthrown quickly after my arrival.

SALOME: Overthrown – and killed?

WILD MAN: Yes, Salome. They are so hated that I could not save them even if I wished.

SALOME: And me? Am I hated too?

WILD MAN: The young and beautiful are not hated, Salome. The people like to think you are on their side – that you have turned against your mother for deserting your father, and that you hate your stepfather.

SALOME: The people might not be altogether wrong, for once.

WILD MAN: And if you joined the revolution the people would love you, not only in Galilee, but everywhere in Palestine.

SALOME [*absently*]: I'm sure they would. . . . Tell me, wild man. When you suppose I would help you to murder my mother, you are counting a little on the Herod blood in me, are you not . . . my holy wild man?

WILD MAN [*steadfastly*]: Once you are baptized you have no such mother as Herodias. She is a stranger to you, and the death she has deserved will leave you indifferent.

SALOME: I begin to see the point about baptism. . . . But tell me, wild man, do you think you can win?

WILD MAN: The revolution will triumph in Galilee within about a week of my return. On the news of the death of the Tetrarch all Palestine will rise. Jerusalem will be in our hands before a month is out. Pontius Pilate will be surrounded in Caesarea. . . .

SALOME [*softly*]: *Surrounded?* Not crushed? Not captured? Not even besieged?

WILD MAN: Caesarea is a great imperial port. Its inhabitants are corrupted. And we have no siege engines.

SALOME: Why not make some?

WILD MAN: We cannot begin making them until we have some free territory.

SALOME: And while you are beginning, new Roman legions will be landing at Caesarea?

WILD MAN: Yes. We have to run that risk.

SALOME: You do, but do I?

WILD MAN: Yes, if you want to live, not just to survive.

SALOME: Live in history, you mean? As a sort of metaphor?

WILD MAN: No, really live, as the person you could be, the person you cannot help wanting to be: not survive into being a cruel painted animal, like Herodias.

SALOME: A short life, then?

WILD MAN: They will repress this particular rising. But it will prepare the way for one they will not repress.

SALOME: But we shall be dead, then. . . .

WILD MAN: We must die anyway, Salome. But this way we shall live before we die.

SALOME: You don't want me to think it out, wild man?

WILD MAN: No, Salome, it is very simple.

SALOME: Then I must dance it out, wild man.
   [SALOME's *third dance is simply expressive of the joy of living, and of curiosity. The* WILD MAN *watches her intently. As she stops dancing she faces the* WILD MAN]

WILD MAN: What does the dancing mean, Salome?

SALOME: It means that I love life, wild man.

WILD MAN: Then you must be on our side, Salome! I shall baptize you!

SALOME: Not here, wild man. In Galilee . . . [*A pause*] Galilee is the place for baptism.

WILD MAN: Then you will join me in Galilee, Salome?

SALOME: Yes, wild man. [*A pause*] I shall join you in Galilee. [*A pause*] In a month's time I shall be in the Tetrarch's palace. When you get there you will send me a message . . .

WILD MAN [*triumphantly*]: And you will give the signal for the rising, Salome!

SALOME [*gravely*]: I shall give the signal, wild man. . . . And now I think it would be best for you to leave this place. The policeman is frightened for the moment and will let you go. But in a little while he will find something else to be frightened of. His instinct tells him to kill you. He knows the arguments *against* killing you, but policemen are always liable to forget that kind of argument. [*She takes his hands. Tenderly*] So go, dear wild man. We shall meet in Galilee . . .

WILD MAN [*solemnly, looking into her eyes*]: In the hour of our life, Salome. The hour for which all men will remember us.

SALOME [*smiling, letting go his hands*]: Hurry, wild man! You have an appointment to keep in Galilee.

WILD MAN: In Galilee, Salome!
[*Exit the* WILD MAN. SALOME *looks after him impassively. Then she begins to dance. The dance begins like the previous one, but then takes a cruel and triumphant turn. During the dance,* PHILO *enters. He is a weary, bedraggled figure with blood on his face, in sharp contrast with the dapper personage of the opening scene. He watches* SALOME'S *dance. She raises her hands as if holding an object, perhaps a head*]

PHILO: Salome! [SALOME *stops dancing and faces* PHILO. *She laughs*]

SALOME: Well, Sophist, so you've found the answer to your question! What is freedom? Freedom is what you have when the police let you go.

PHILO [*ignoring the sarcasm*]: Where is the wild man?

SALOME: Not to worry, Sophist. The wild man has left town. And I am going to follow him.

PHILO: Where?

SALOME: Galilee.

PHILO: Why?
H.—H

SALOME: Politics.

PHILO: Whose?

SALOME: His.

PHILO: How?

SALOME: Perfidiously.

PHILO: How much?

SALOME: Fatally.

PHILO: To whom?

SALOME: Him.

PHILO: By whom?

SALOME: Me.

PHILO: Why?

SALOME: Life.

PHILO: Whose?

SALOME: Mine.

PHILO [*thoughtfully*]: It is your idea then, that life requires you to betray?

SALOME: Life *is* betrayal. What survives has always betrayed that which did not survive. As you know, Sophist.

PHILO: As *I* know?

SALOME: When we danced together, the wild man and I, you took fright and went down to the police station. In order to survive, by means of betraying.

PHILO: That was forced on me.

SALOME [*defiantly and rather brittly*]: Yes. You are barely a survivor. But when *I* betray it is because I choose to do so. I shall go to Galilee, I shall trap the wild man and kill him. Not because I have to, but because I [*a suggestion of a catch in her voice*] want to.

PHILO: Nobody just wants to. Something makes you want to. What?

SALOME [*loudly*]: Justice.

PHILO [*startled*]: *Justice?*

SALOME [*angrily*]: The justice he wants. The justice you cannot live with. The justice of the dead. He is death. He has called me. But I am not coming. What is coming is what he really wants. What I am going to give him. His death. I shall dance and he will die. We shall both be doing what we want to do. Not what is forced on us, as sophists do. We are free people. [*Her voice trembles*] We shall make an enviable couple. [*A pause*]

PHILO: He has chosen death. We know he will bear it bravely. You have chosen life. How will you bear that?

SALOME: As my grandfather did. Bravely, splendidly, cruelly. And in the end horribly.
[*A pause*]

PHILO: So we both betray the wild man.

SALOME: Betray, Sophist? I thought you were his open enemy.

PHILO: Yes. I can betray him all the same, by doing what he does not expect even of his enemy.

SALOME: And what is that, dear teacher, smug old Sophist?

PHILO: You can only betray his body, Salome. I betray his spirit. It is what we call interpretation. Let me see. . . . He returns to Galilee. You decoy him into a trap. The Tetrarch has him killed. So far so good. Right, Salome? [SALOME *nods*] And then, Salome? What do you do with the martyr? How do you face him? [SALOME *moves her feet*] You can dance, Salome. But the Romans will have to send in troops. And still more troops to fight the ghost of the martyr. That is why they will have to call on me.

SALOME: To fight, Sophist?

PHILO: With my proper weapons. With words. I shall
capture the wild man once you have killed him. He will
remain brave and virtuous, as he was in life. His cult will
be encouraged. But his message will be changed. He will
have become a quiet Galilean. Not a revolutionary, but a
spiritual and ethical reformer. A somewhat ethereal pillar of
the Empire. This we can organize. It is called historiography.

SALOME: I am for survival, Sophist, I suppose, and you are
for . . .?

PHILO: Civilization, Salome. We are on the same side.

SALOME: I am sorry I had to have you beaten up, Philo.

PHILO: I bear no malice, Salome. Except in a universal sense,
of course.

SALOME: We are lonely, you and I, Philo. We must stick
together.

PHILO: Yes, Salome. That is why we are lonely.

SALOME: No, Philo. We are lonely for what we have lost.
We are lonely for what I must kill and you must bury. We
are lonely for what cannot be killed and cannot be buried.
You are lonely for the difficult student, and most lonely
in your dreary, clever revenge: I am lonely for what might
have been a comrade and what might have been a lover. I
am lonely for the journey I must make into Galilee, towards
a meeting which will leave me more lonely than ever. It
is very simple, Philo, however we say it. We are lonely for
the wild man.

PHILO: Yes, Salome. We are lonely for him. And yet we
cannot get rid of him. We kill him, we bury him, we even
honour him. And yet he always comes up again under a
new name.

SALOME: We shall always be lonely, my dear Philo, so let
us dance together, we survivors, in our civilized way. [*They
begin to dance decorously together*] We need not be sorry for
him. He will always have company.
    [*Fade*]

CURTAIN

King Herod Advises

Cast

HEROD

SALO ME, his granddaughter and assistant

AN T-AIRE UISGE FE THALAMH, Minister for Underground Development

MAJOR AUGHILLY AUGHRIM OF AHOGHILL

AN T-ATHAIR AFANÁIS O H-UALLAIGH, Father Athanasius Woolley

Performed at the Peacock Theatre.
Dublin, in 1973.

King Herod Advises

Scene

What looks like a rather far-out psychoanalyst's consulting room, fitted out in vaguely oriental style. A large picture of the Temple (reconstructed) at Jerusalem: Another of the Wailing Wall: A sign reading Dr H. E. Rodd Ph.D. (Jerusalem), M.D. (Vienna), Litt.D. (Dublin).

HEROD *at his desk: he is in formal dress, in contrast with the slightly eccentric décor. He is reading a newspaper with Arabic characters. He is smiling with satisfaction.*

HEROD: Good, very good. [*He picks up a* New York Times, *looks through it quickly and chuckles*] Better still! [*He picks up an* Irish Times, *turns to the editorial page and laughs aloud*] Great stuff! [*Enter his assistant,* SALOME, *an attractive girl dressed like a nurse*] The news is absolutely splendid, Salome, my dear, all over the place! Fantastic some of the things they think up in September 1969.

SALOME [*businesslike*]: The Minister is here to see you.

HEROD: Which Minister?

SALOME: He said to say just the Minister.

HEROD: Oh, that one. Show him in. [*As she goes out*] Just the Minister indeed! Just the Minister for *me*. [*Re-enter* SALOME]

SALOME [*with a good blas*★]: An t-Aire Uisge fe Thalamh, the Minister for Underground Development.
　　Enter AN T-AIRE UISGE FE THALAMH, *a dapper little man wearing a green carnation:* HEROD *rises and bows*]

MINISTER [*placing his hands on the back of a chair and declaiming*]: *There's nothing but our own red blood Can make a right Rose-tree!*

HEROD [*opening a drawer and taking from it a large butcher's knife. In a tone of polite enquiry as if taking an order*]: Your *own* red blood, Minister?

★ Gaelic accent.

MINISTER [*sitting down and lighting a cigarette, waving aside the question*]: Well, someone's.

[HEROD *bows again, replaces the knife on the desk and sits down*]

HEROD: Your Excellency, I understand, has a problem which you think may fall into my – er – domain? 'Field', they say these days.

MINISTER: It's about the freedom-fighters in the North.

HEROD: What about them?

MINISTER: They won't fight.

HEROD: Let me get this straight. The freedom-fighters in the North are not fighting for freedom in the North. Right?

MINISTER: Right.

HEROD [*gravely*]: That's bad, Minister. In fact it's downright illogical. But why is this happening, or rather failing to happen?

MINISTER: Their leaders are a bunch of Marxists.

HEROD [*astonished*]: Marxists, your Excellency? What do you mean by that?

MINISTER [*impatiently*]: I mean *Marxists*, of course. Followers of Karl Marx. Bloody Commies.

HEROD: Not bloody enough, it seems. But about Marx. You astonish me. Salome! The special Register, please. Volume MAN–MAY.

MINISTER [*exasperated*]: Dr Rodd, let's stop beating about the bush.

HEROD [*with an air of authority*]: Minister, in your own office you are the boss. Indeed, if what they tell me is true, you are the boss in quite a few other people's offices too. . . . But when you put yourself in the hands of a specialist, then *he* is the boss.

[*Enter* SALOME *with a large volume which* HEROD *takes from her*]

*H

HEROD : Here we are. Yes, as I thought. Exceptionally high
ratings all round. In *class*-hate of course he gets Alpha
plus plus plus. Marvellous! But well up the field in *national*
hate too – says some splendid things about the Russians.
That's good, eh! [*Chuckles*] Makes the grade on race-hate –
insulting an opponent for his Negroid appearance – good,
good. One of the most eminent of Jewish anti-Semites – a
man after my own heart really! [*Looking up from the volume*]
Your Excellency, I simply cannot see what fault you can
possibly have to find with Karl Marx!

MINISTER : He was a non-Catholic.

HEROD [*handing the volume to* SALOME]: Take him away.
[*To* MINISTER, *thoughtfully*] You know, of all the things
that have been said and written about Karl Marx what you
have said is probably the most profound.

MINISTER [*modestly*]: Oh, I don't know.

HEROD : Yes, yes. You don't just want hate. You want
Catholic hate.

MINISTER [*primly*]: Catholics aren't supposed to hate people.

HEROD : You could have fooled me.

MINISTER : *They* hate *us*. *We* defend ourselves against *them*.

HEROD [*nodding*]: Classical. Sound. *They* say the same of
course, so nobody hates anyone. My practice should be
in ruins, but I get along somehow, I get along. Why call
it hate, why not call it defence, justice or simply love?
What's in a name? Tell me, Minister, you are a rich man,
are you not?

MINISTER : I am a philanthropist. I contribute to various
charities.

HEROD : Quite so. Is it your experience, being a rich man,
that people hate you for that?

MINISTER : A few people say they do. Most people don't.

HEROD [*nodding*]: Why don't they?

MINISTER: They want to be rich themselves. Some of them hope to get away with it, and admire people who do get away with it. The rest have just given up and don't care one way or another.

HEROD: But supposing – just supposing – that I were a prominent powerful rich man in this city, with a finger in every pie as they say, a Minister-businessman, would people hate *me*?

MINISTER: Of course they would.

HEROD: Why?

MINISTER: Because you're a Jew.

HEROD: And you're *not* a Jew?

MINISTER [*indignantly*]: Jesus, no!

HEROD: A devastating analysis of classical Marxism, Minister. Class-hate is not enough!

MINISTER: Class-hate is immoral.

HEROD: How true! It can also be impractical. That is your problem about the freedom-fighters, or the non-freedom-non-fighters, is it not, Minister?

MINISTER: They haven't *done* anyone in years.

HEROD: You have defined the problem. How many people do you *want* them to 'do'?

MINISTER: They shall be remembered forever.

HEROD: Which ones? The ones who get done, or the ones who do them?

MINISTER: The nation's honour is dearer than the nation's life.

HEROD: Nation's honours come pretty dear all right. [*Businesslike*] And what do *you* get out of it, Minister?

MINISTER: Ask not what my country shall do for me. Ask only who I shall do for my country.

HEROD: Well, who *someone* will do for *something*. What's your something?

MINISTER: The resumption of the national advance.

HEROD: What about it?

MINISTER: It calls for sacrifices from us all.

HEROD: I am sure it does. And from you in particular?

MINISTER: It calls for the sacrifice of my subordinate status.

HEROD [*pleased*]: Of course. I see. In an *advance* there has to be a *leader*. So . . .

MINISTER: I have heard the call.

HEROD: *You* have heard it. But how many other people have heard you being called? Not quite everybody, eh, Minister?

MINISTER: Well, no.

HEROD: So something to make them hear it? Like a Big Bang up there, eh?

MINISTER: Well, yes.

HEROD [*nodding*]: The root of the trouble is clear enough. [*Taking out a piece of paper and beginning to write*] It's a clear case of inhibition of aggression and ambition through the constricting presence of an inappropriate . . . ideology. Here's your prescription [*handing it to him on tip of butcher's knife*]

MINISTER [*reading it*]: Nationalism *plus* Catholicism *plus* money *plus* arms *minus* Marxism *equals* a solution.

HEROD [*rises*]: A provisional solution, of course. You will forgive me, Minister; other patients, you know [*pressing bell*].

MINISTER: Thank you, Dr Rodd. Your services will not be forgotten on the Day.

HEROD [*coldly*]: I am already an honorary Aryan. But I shall buy a *Fainne*.★ [*Exit* MINISTER *with* SALOME. *Noise of a slight scuffle.* SALOME *returns, flushed*]

SALOME: What a horrible man!

HEROD: Tautology, Salome. Man is horrible. He is a man. Therefore he is horrible. What did he do?

SALOME: He asked me where I learned my Irish. Then he pinched my bottom.

HEROD: Reminds me [*smiling reminiscently*] of the worst excesses of the Roman Empire. My best period. What else did he do?

SALOME: He said he liked plump little Jewesses.

HEROD [*nodding*]: Broadminded of him. Taking care of his liberal image, no doubt. [*Patting her on the shoulder*] Don't worry about him, Salome. We are not likely to see him again. He thinks he is cleverer than someone else, who is in fact cleverer than he is, and that is always unfortunate. Mark Anthony was the same. Except that *he* liked plump little Egyptians. There has to be some way of telling all these fellows apart. Next patient?

SALOME [*reading with difficulty*]: Major Aughilly Aughrim of Ahoghill.

HEROD: Oh dear, and so soon after lunch. Show him in.
     [*She brings in* MAJOR AUGHRIM, *a big man with a wooden, glazed expression, holding a bowler hat in his hands. He shakes hands with Herod without speaking and sits down*]

HEROD: Your trouble, Major?

MAJOR A.: Trouble? The Romans, of course!

HEROD [*incredulously*]: Romans! Salome! [*Enter* SALOME] What century are we in?

SALOME: Twentieth, Christian style, A.D. 1972. Do you want Jewish and Moslem as well?
     [HEROD *waves negatively. Exit* SALOME]

★ Gold lapel-ring, signifying that the wearer is a Gaelic-speaker.

HEROD: Major Aughrim, *I* had trouble with Romans. That was in the first century. How can you be still having trouble with Romans?

MAJOR A.: Holy Romans, I mean.

HEROD [*even more astonished*]: Romans *holy*! That's new.

MAJOR A.: For God's sake, Doctor, it's the Roman Catholics are the trouble; I want ye to give me something for them.

HEROD [*nodding*]: Now I understand, Major, and I sympathize. Roman Catholics indeed! I've just met one. How many of them do *you* seem to have?

MAJOR A. [*eagerly*]: At least five hundred thousand of them, Doctor, and they're breeding all the time, and there's more next door.

HEROD: My God!

MAJOR A.: My God is right, Doctor, and you don't know the half of it. They're out of their minds! They want to drive the Protestants out of Ulster!

HEROD: And what do *you* want to do?

MAJOR A.: I want to drive the Catholics out of Ulster, like any sane man.

HEROD [*nodding*]: A clear-cut situation. You know, Major, that I am a Jew myself!

MAJOR A. [*warmly*]: If you came to Ulster, Doctor, I assure you that we Protestants would welcome you as a fellow-Christian!

HEROD: Thank you, Major. That is very . . . Christian of you.

MAJOR A.: We're not bigoted, the way people say we are. It's just the Roman Catholics are more than flesh and blood can stand.

HEROD: I don't know if I understand the subtleties of your position fully, Major, but it seems to me that you would like to eliminate what I might call the Roman Catholic presence from your body politic?

MAJOR A.: We want rid of them once and for all, and that's a fact.

HEROD: And what's stopping you?

MAJOR A.: The British Army, that's what. We're loyalists, and we don't want to fight the British Army.

HEROD: Loyalists. . . . Loyal to what?

MAJOR A.: Loyal to the British Crown, of course.

HEROD: This British Army is the Army of the British Crown, is it not?

MAJOR A.: Of course.

HEROD: So you insist on being loyal to the institution which is preventing you from doing what you want to do?
    [MAJOR A. *seems to be suffering from thought*]
Funny thing, you know, your trouble is fundamentally the same as that of the patient who has just left.

MAJOR A. [*nervously*]: What was up with him?

HEROD: The same that's up with you. Oh, the symptoms are superficially quite different. My last patient was, well, not of the same . . . way of thinking as yourself.

MAJOR A. [*alarmed*]: You don't mean he was . . .?

HEROD: I fear so. Mind you, he didn't tell me so in so many words, but there was something about him, something, well . . . Roman!

MAJOR A. [*pushing his chair back in alarm*]: Doctor, is it here you saw him? [*Lowering his voice*] Could it . . . could it be catching?

HEROD: Calm yourself, Major. Catholicism, like the other forms of Christianity, can indeed be contagious under certain conditions but you are quite safe. It is clear to my professional eye that you have been adequately immunized against the Roman virus. No, what you have in common with my last patient . . . [*The* MAJOR *looks like protesting but* HEROD *quells him with a gesture*] is quite different. The trouble in both cases has to be defined as follows – now listen carefully to my diagnosis. [*The* MAJOR *leans forward attentively:* HEROD *speaks slowly*] Chronic inhibition of aggressive impulse due to the presence in the affected area of an inappropriate ideology.

MAJOR A. [*frowning*]: Inappropriate . . .?

HEROD: Ideology, Major, ideology.

MAJOR A.: Is that serious?

HEROD: Serious but not fatal. In the nature of the disease it is the *cure* that is fatal. But to someone else. [MAJOR *again strives to utter, but is quelled*] In the case of my last patient the inhibiting ideology – of which the carriers were persons other than himself – was Marxism. . . . Marxism! I gave him a prescription enabling him to eliminate this and he is now a happier man, exploding every day as regularly as clockwork. I can fix you up the same way. [*Begins to write*]

MAJOR A.: You have me a wee bit confused, Doctor. [HEROD *continues to write*]

HEROD: Major, you were confused when you came in. Now you *understand* that you are confused. That is progress. [*Finishes writing and looks at prescription*] In your case, Major, the inhibiting factor is not Marxism. No, no. It is loyalism.

MAJOR A. [*shocked*]: Loyalism!

HEROD [*firmly*]: Loyalism: that is, the condition of being a loyalist. That is what you must eliminate. Here is my prescription. [*Skewers prescription on butcher's knife and presents it to* MAJOR A. *who takes it and reads*]

MAJOR A. [*reading*]: Ulster Protestantism *plus* Ulster Nationalism *minus* British loyalism *plus* money *plus* arms equals the cure for your trouble! . . . I don't understand, Doctor.

HEROD: Major, I know you don't claim to be an intellectual but I really must ask you now to make an effort at cerebration. Just this once. I'll try to stimulate you. [*Speaking*

slowly] Major! How can you – you of all people – be
loyal – *loyal* – to people who are protecting Roman
Catholics – protecting Roman Catholics? Don't you see
that if you remain loyal in this way *you are yourself helping
to protect Roman Catholics?*
[*A pause*]

MAJOR A.: My God! You're right, Doctor, you're right!
That's what loyalty means today all right.
[HEROD *mops his brow with a silk handkerchief of oriental
design*]
If the Army go on standing between us and the Fenians
we'll make it hot for them till they get out and leave the
Fenians to us. Then we'll teach them a lesson they won't
forget.

HEROD [*with lassitude*]: You're well on the way to a cure,
Major. Before long we'll have you exploding as regularly
as my last patient. [*Rises*] Well, goodbye, Major. Good
hunting, perhaps I should say.

MAJOR A. [*fiercely military demeanour*]: Up Ulster!
[*He leaves, forgetting his bowler hat*]

HEROD [*meditatively*]: Up Ulster . . . [*He picks up his butcher's
knife and examines its edge. Enter* SALOME. HEROD *puts down
his knife*] Well, my dear, any pinches this time?

SALOME: No, he just said if I'd come to . . . Ahoghill, he'd
show me he was no bigot. [*She hands* HEROD *a card*]

HEROD: He probably isn't by the standards of Ahoghill.
[*Looking at the card*] What's this, I can't read it.

SALOME: It's in Gaelic. He's a priest.

HEROD [*putting down the card*]: Gaelic, I see. His real name is
probably something quite simple, like Tom Gill. Where did
you put him?

SALOME: The room across the corridor. I didn't want the
Major to meet him.

HEROD: Good girl. Well, bring in the holy man. [*Exit*

SALOME. *To the audience*] I get on well enough with priests, you know. Oh, they denounce me and all that, especially around Christmas. Indeed I'm supposed to be a bit of an ogre [*brandishing his butcher's knife in mock ferocity*]. But in practice, we get along, we get along, the Church and I.
 Re-enter SALOME *with* AN T-ATHAIR AFANÁIS O H-UALLAIGH. AN T-ATHAIR *is in his early thirties: he wears a black polo-necked sweater and a rather tentative beard; he is thin and anxious*]

HEROD [*taking the priest's hand*]: Father . . .? [*Groping for the name*]

FATHER WOOLLEY: An t-Athair O h-Uallaigh, Doctor.

HEROD: Of course, of course.

FATHER W.: Father Woolley.
 [*Re-enter Major Aughrim*]

MAJOR A.: Excuse me, Doctor. My hat. [*Collecting the bowler. To* AN T-ATHAIR] Very sorry to interrupt the consultation. [*Looking curiously and a little anxiously at* AN T-ATHAIR]

HEROD [*introducing*]: Major Aughrim. [*Hurriedly*] Doctor Woolley.

FATHER W. [*puzzled*]: I'm not a doctor, Doctor. I'm a . . .
 [*As* MAJOR A. *puts his head on one side, looking at* FATHER WOOLLEY *intently*, HEROD *takes the* MAJOR *and steers him to the door, talking fast and breezily*]

HEROD: Of course, of course, quite right – you're a patient, not a doctor, a patient [*almost shouting*] the doctor–patient relation, you know, not a doctor–doctor relation, goodbye, Major, *goodbye*.
 [*Exit* MAJOR A. HEROD *again wipes his forehead with his oriental handkerchief*]

HEROD: Funny thing, Father. That man hates your cloth, as they say. But then, you're not wearing your cloth, are you? Very sensible, as it turns out. [*Businesslike*] Now, Father, your . . . difficulty?

FATHER W.: Well, it's this, Doctor. The . . . insurgents
in the North, I'm told they are fighting for a better society,
a more Christian one. I feel . . . in a way that . . . perhaps
I should be with them.

HEROD [*briskly*]: So what's stopping you?

FATHER W.: [*in a low voice*]: Some of the things they do.

HEROD [*sitting at his desk, using a slightly bored, clinical tone,
writing on a pad*]: Let me see now. You experience difficulties
in approving certain things. Legitimation–obstruction, we
call that, but never mind the jargon. Let's just see where it
hurts. [*Abruptly*] Shooting a British soldier. That bother you?

FATHER W.: Well, I suppose that's war, anyway.

HEROD [*nodding and writing*]: Acceptable level. Shooting a
policeman, then?

FATHER W. [*reluctantly*]: I suppose that's war too . . .

HEROD [*looking at him thoughtfully, then writing again*]: Threshold
near. So then. Shooting an unarmed policeman in the
presence of his family?

FATHER W.: No!

HEROD: I see. Well, the rest follows, doesn't it? You jib at that,
you jib also at car-bombs, bombs in public places, booby-
traps and also at all the apparatus of revolutionary justice:
shooting through both knee-caps, tarring and feathering
of women and girls, and so forth and so on?

FATHER W.: All that is terrible, unspeakable. . . .

HEROD [*cutting him short*]: In short, you jib. [*Getting up and
walking around his desk*] Come, Father, your problem is
really very simple. These people are fighting for a more
Christian society. Right?

FATHER W. [*with a trace of hesitation*]: Yes . . . I believe
they are.

HEROD: And, for you, as a Christian, a more Christian
society means a more just society. Right?

FATHER W.: Of course.

HEROD: A war to achieve a just society is a *just war!*
[AN T-ATHAIR *tries to speak but* HEROD *waves him to silence*]
The Church has always allowed that there are just wars. The Church in every nation has always blessed just wars, that is every war in which that particular nation happened to engage. Voltaire went into all that. The fact that a war is horrible, unspeakable and so on doesn't mean that it is not a *just* war. The same things happen in a just war as in any other war. What is Belfast compared with Hiroshima, Nagasaki, Dresden, Hanoi? Why, compared with the late Harry Truman and the living Dick Nixon, your poor little John Stephenson is practically a pacifist! You know, really, Father, people who have no trouble accepting Truman and Nixon, and make a great fuss about Mr Stephenson being a terrorist are not proving how much they hate violence – they're just proving what snobs they are. Violence, you know, is like trade. Retail violence is socially unacceptable. [*He picks up his butcher's knife with disdain*] The wholesale kind is entirely respectable. [*He holds his butcher's knife like a sceptre, radiating rectitude*]

FATHER W. [*speaking with conviction*]: Doctor, you mis-understand my case completely. I *don't* accept the idea of the just war. That idea is now theologically discredited. [HEROD *drops his butcher's knife in alarm*] I *don't* approve of what Truman did to Hiroshima or Nixon to Hanoi. I find all that unspeakable.

HEROD [*shaken and agitated for the first time*]: Theologically discredited! The just war! Why it's like learning of the sudden death of a dear old friend! [*Looking at* AN T-ATHAIR *with rising aversion*] Your case, my friend, is much more serious than I thought. In fact, I don't like the look of it at all. [*Pacing the room moodily, then brightly*] Maybe, maybe. You know, it might work. It might be the answer. The answer in terms of legitimation theory. The answer!

FATHER W.: The answer to what?

HEROD: The answer to the death of the just war!

FATHER W.: And what is the answer?

HEROD [*solemnly*]: Institutionalized violence!

FATHER W. [*thoughtfully*]: You know, I don't think I understand what that means.

HEROD [*severely*]: Then it's time you got wise to it, Father. Do you know where they're all talking about institutionalized violence now? County Mayo – there's where! And they wouldn't talk about it if they didn't know what it meant, would they now?

FATHER W. [*doubtfully but charitably*]: I suppose not.

HEROD: Well, then, let me show you how this works. It's really rather beautiful, and if you follow it carefully you will be completely cured. Now listen. Every society has laws, right? [AN T-ATHAIR *nods to these rhetorical questions as they come*] And in every society there are injustices, right? And the laws uphold the injustices, right? Good. Next step. In every society there is a police force and an army. Right? They are prepared to use violence. Right? They will use violence against any attempt to change the laws, right?

FATHER W.: Not quite. Against any attempt to change the laws *by force*. In our kind of society they can be changed otherwise, democratically.

HEROD: Not in Northern Ireland, they couldn't. And are you really saying the laws of your democratic republic are *just*? Are you? Just to the poor? Just to the unemployed? Just to the itinerant? Just to women?

FATHER W.: No, Certainly not.

HEROD: The laws here are unjust and your democracy does nothing to change them.

FATHER W.: Not 'nothing'. Just – not enough.

HEROD [*sourly*]: Yours is a serious case, Father. You must really cooperate more with your physician. Once again.

The laws are unjust. The parliament does not change them.
And if people break these unjust laws what will happen
then?

FATHER W.: The police will arrest them.

HEROD: And if there are too many for the police to arrest?

FATHER W.: Then I suppose the Army would intervene.

HEROD: Intervene! Another snobbish phrase. What you
mean is the soldiers will bash and kill people, and go on
bashing and killing them until the poor lie down again.
Isn't that the reality of it?

FATHER W. [*reluctantly*]: Yes, I'm afraid it is.

HEROD: So. We're making progress. We have established,
with your agreement, the *existence* of institutionalized
violence. From there on it's plain sailing. Since violence is
institutionalized, and pervades and sustains all the institutions
of the state, there is no point in talking about *using* violence
or not using it. . . . When you sit there quiet as a mouse,
in appearance, in your little presbytery you are in reality
using violence all the time, since you acquiesce in the laws
and police which prevent poor people from occupying your
spare room.

FATHER W.: Well, not exactly. At the moment my spare
room is occupied by an itinerant family.

HEROD [*exasperated*]: Father Woolley, you are an
exceptionally difficult patient. Who is or is not in your spare
room is completely irrelevant. The point is that the occupants
know that, *if you wanted to*, you could at any moment call the
police and put them out. They are therefore the victims
of *latent* institutionalized violence, in which you are an
implicit accomplice. It's hard to be patient with such
villainy! You show yourself very queasy about 'men of
violence', Father, but you are really a practitioner of violence
yourself, disguising it as charity.

[*A pause.* FATHER WOOLLEY *is silent, his head bowed*]
Good. So what is the relation of what the snobs call

'terrorism' to all this? There is the nub of the matter.
Institutionalized violence is primary violence, all-pervasive
violence, the permanent violent aggression of the rich against
the poor. The poor have the right to defend themselves
against this permanent aggression. And since the poor are
too helpless, too dispirited, to defend themselves, others
– even not so poor – may undertake their defence. These
brave defenders are the men you call terrorists. Just as the
regular Army when it 'intervenes', as you call it, uses means
appropriate to its situation and resources, from CS gas
up to nuclear weapons, so your so-called terrorist uses
means appropriate to *his* situation and resources. One of
the most effective of these has been found to be the time-
bomb planted in a public place. This, of course, produces
innocent victims. That is the accepted risk of any military
operation, including the 'intervention' of the regular forces.
But the so-called terrorist himself is not responsible for this.
What is responsible is *institutionalized violence* of which the
bomb in the supermarket and the beggar's hungry child
are just different end-products. When the bomb explodes
in the supermarket, *both* the bomber *and* those who are
killed are the victims of institutionalized violence. The
criminal responsible *is the supermarket itself.* The supermarket
represents the flaunted arrogance of the acquisitive society,
backed by the police and ultimately the army of that
society. So when the supermarket . . . blows itself up, that
is something to rejoice at. It is the society of institutionalized
violence beginning to commit suicide. It is your more just
society beginning to emerge. And remember it is the old,
unjust society which is responsible for imposing *all* the
suffering with which that emergence is attended. Do you
follow me?

FATHER W.: I think so.

HEROD [*beaming*]: Excellent! You're ticking away, ticking
away. [*Writing*] This will be my third cure of the day.
Provided you follow this prescription. Let me read you the
prescription. 'As often as you say your prayers every day,
and when you have finished your prayers every day, repeat

three times the blessed and salutary words: "Institutionalized violence".' There!

[*Skewering the prescription on the knife and holding it out to* FATHER WOOLLEY, *who does not hold out his hand*]

FATHER W.: No, Doctor. I'm afraid I cannot follow that prescription or your advice.

HEROD [*puts down the knife. In a 'back to the drawing board' tone*]: So what's wrong with it? Too logical? Is that it? You Micks don't like logic much, do you?

FATHER W. [*shrugging*]: Not much. Not if it leads to conclusions we don't like. We're like other people.

HEROD: Uh-huh. Should have been woollier. [*Writing*] Father Woolley says – 'make it woollier!' Ha ha. Also leave out the concrete examples – supermarket etc. With a few alterations I'll get some of your colleagues to follow my prescription.

FATHER W.: Thank you, Doctor. You have made some things clearer.

HEROD [*suspiciously*]: What things, like?

FATHER W.: You said, there is institutionalized violence in *all* societies. That made me think. So if the bombers win . . . there will still be institutionalized violence. And why should I ever have thought that the violence would be less barbaric when re-institutionalized by the kind of people who plant bombs in supermarkets? Should I have thought they were fighting for the poor? If they win they'll be rich. Already their leaders are not poor, and most of the people they hurt and kill *are* poor. We should be going back, not forward. I should have seen that for myself earlier. But you see, Doctor, I have a brother in the Movement. Thank you, Doctor. You have helped me in your way; you were so lucid, and so calm. Good evening.

[*He holds out his hand.* HEROD *bows stiffly. As* FATHER WOOLLEY *leaves,* HEROD *mutters*]

HEROD: Frankly, I prefer the Pharisees.
[*He tears up the prescription refused by* FATHER WOOLLEY.
Enter SALOME. *She holds an evening paper*]

HEROD [*with lassitude*]: Well, my dear, that's our last client
for today. [*Looking at her*] He left your bottom undented,
I imagine?

SALOME: He is a shy man. And a good man, I think.

HEROD [*as if examining the idea*]: A *good* man? A good *man*?
A *good man?* Could that be, Salome?

SALOME: Grandfather, I wish you could think so.

HEROD: It's been a long day, Salome. I would have liked to
be going home now. [*He opens the drawer and carefully puts
back the butcher's knife, closes the drawer and sits down at his
desk. He closes his eyes for a moment, then re-opens them*]
What was in the evening paper?

SALOME: I just saw the headlines – 'Quiet day in Belfast'.
[*She hands him the paper.* HEROD *takes it and reads*]

HEROD [*in a flat voice*]: Small explosion in Donegall Street;
one infant killed by flying glass.
[*He puts down the paper and closes his eyes again. The stage
darkens. The same sound of a baby crying as in* King Herod
Explains. HEROD *has his face in his hands. Light on* SALOME]

SALOME [*to the audience*]: So what is Herod about, you ask?
You have a nerve. You know damn well what Herod is
about, each one of you.
Oh, not that you kill people, most of you –
You don't have that much nerve.
You don't kill people, you just set it up for them.
The Minister we saw first, it was you who made him
possible –
You and your old nonsense that you only half pretend to
believe in.
That Fourth Green Field that you long for so much –
In a pig's eye you long for it!
You'd build a wall to keep it out if you could!

But you let people keep on saying you had to have it
Until the Provos finally went to get it for you, the only way
they know.
And then you said how terrible it was all those poor people
being killed in the North and when would it all end?
   [HEROD *has his face in his hands*]
Poor Grandfather!
It's you who keep him alive, of course.
You like to have a kind of ogre around, a heavy for
Christmas.
Prowling about, making your flesh creep, you poor innocent
lambs.
It's all part of the same game.
Cruelty and violence are supposed to be outside you.
They have the face of the stranger, the man of
an alien religion, the incomprehensible, the monster:
Herod on the one hand,
And you, the Innocents, on the other:
Just like that.
Cosy, isn't it?
Major Aughrim sees it the same way: he just uses a
different dialect, which sounds funny to you –
Or sounded funny.
The deep pool of your self-righteousness from time
to time spills over in murder.
And then you point the finger at Herod!
You hypocrites!
You snivelling, cowardly, complacent, craw-thumping,
flag-waving, sneaking –

HEROD [*opening his eyes*] Salome, my dear.

SALOME: Yes, Grandfather.

HEROD: Don't out-Herod Herod!

SALOME: Sorry, Grandfather.

HEROD: The trouble about telling other people not to be
   self-righteous is that you wind up by being self-righteous
   yourself.

[*To audience*] Don't mind my granddaughter.
You're no worse than I am.
I understand you.
I'm not a pacifist, you know.
Never have been.
But I thought that since you insist on keeping Herod around
As the morbid part of the entertainment, the gruesome
object in the holly –
That it might be to the point to show you where to
look for me.
Not just in the holly and not just at Christmas
But in – how shall I put it – the permanent ingenuity of
your own aggressivity!
That is what you have to look out for if you really
want to end the violence, which between ourselves I beg
leave to doubt.
I had to show you that.
I, Herod, who am also Everyman
I who have both suffered and inflicted pain
Herod, the husband of Mariamne
Herod, the father of Alexander and Aristobulus
I, Herod, since you will always think the worst of me
Took up my butcher's knife and played the Tempter.
The Evil One.
The Wandering Jew, who by definition is up to no good.
So I showed you a Minister and a major and I also showed
you a priest. That priest got away – somewhat to my
surprise.
But I could easily have shown you priests who did not get
away.
Priests hooked forever on drugged words
Incurable addicts in their cells of sophistry
With their genuine compassion turned inside out and
converted into callousness
Muttering in their moral sleep that spell of Circe:
'Institutionalized violence'.
Oh, and I could have shown you others – plenty of others.
Editors for example.
I thought of showing you an editor. I thought seriously

about that.

But then I said to myself: 'Herod, my friend, don't you
get a bad enough press as it is?'

But before I played my own part as Tempter I read the
editorials.

I liked particularly all the ones that said:

'We cannot condone violence but . . .'

But

The butt of a gun.

I admired the unbroken flow of smooth abstraction
around the general idea of violence.

I admired the unshakable confidence that the ideas
current in *our* tribe were the only correct ideas.

And that the failure of the other tribe to absorb these
self-evident correct ideas was at the root of the violence.

Theirs *not* ours. The guilt for all is theirs alone.

Blessed are the communicators for they shall convince
themselves of their own righteousness!

Let ye be going home now and leave me – to my own
devices.

And remember this: I, Herod the Great always preferred
peace to war.

I never condoned violence but . . .

And it is because of that 'but' that you remember me
today with execration.

So be careful.

CURTAIN